v v v

Footprints Through the Ash

v v v

Front cover source by Bob Hackett 2015087

Preface

Sometimes it feels like the world is burning down around us.
Maybe we caused the fire, or didn't put it out fast enough.
Maybe life is such a mess that there were so many fires it wasn't
even possible to put them all out. Or maybe it was spontaneous
combustion – bursting into the bright cleansing flame of
inspiration.

Whatever the source of the flame – as poets, we use it. These
poems are channeled from the epic hall of emotion that is our
lives. Let the philosophy and tenderness and joy shown here take
you forward, and hopefully help put out a few fires of your own.
Or fan the flames of the good ones.

Poetry is a journey, and we invite you to walk with us. Leave
behind some Footprints through the Ash.

Contents

[S. Libellule]

Footprints Through Ash

I am a most beautiful arsonist
able to light my way
through any dark day
forever igniting
while ever exciting

candles
bridges
desires

such a crazed blaze
having so much fun
yet when all is done
all that is left...
footprints through ash

───────────

Libellule is originally from New England and now lives outside Birmingham, Alabama. The poet writes about nature, authenticity, and the examined life. Influences include Mary Oliver and Billy Collins. Allpoetry.com/Little_Dragonfly

[Ronnie Byron Chambers]

My Rosewood

I built a life from dark circles
red pepper and sea salt
benches of ebony
to visit when dully tired
and too often russet broken branches
like upside down eights
on a hill in a deeper valley
walked and ran
crawled too
in circles and more

circles were friends
till knocking at a door
standing blue eyed brunette
a painting like Picasso
thirty years and three days
passing like yesterday
still smiling demure like Mona Lisa
those eyes colored more topaz
four and flour more added
in a home upon a hill

sixty and three years and a day
still moving up the hill
clothed in obsidian and alabaster lace
planting the burnt umber dirt with her ashes

a Stradivarius violin unstrung
my spruce willow maple ebony and rosewood
still upon my hill

I began writing in 1984 leading me to become a teacher of
literature for thirty years. Also, I am a professional drummer, and
I have a beautiful family which is the highlight of my life.
Allpoetry.com/R_Byron

[Rebecca Friend]

Carolina blue

Dawn breaks in dead silence,
a Carolina morning holding her breath,
waiting with me beside the sea
for earth to stir a breeze,
sunrise spreads a gold band
and peach-pink strands,
like an unfolding fan,
as whitecaps ripple out of reach
on kitty hawk beach.

Beyond my cottage door,
azure waves christen that shore
of shell and sand,
again and again,
a serrated seaside
stenciled by tide,
undisturbed by tourists...
they all flock south like ocean-bound
herring gulls
just to drown
in myrtle beach crowds.

I drift into a postcard memory of
dawn by the sea,
when the air smelled like salt and
lavender rain

and I danced alone on that jewel-toned plane,
southern belle on her stage of
buried pearls and corkscrew curls,
bluejeans and a ballerina's
daydreams,

just a shadow preening on tip-toe,
now stretched into a grey
wisp of a woman,
but as this carolina morning
illuminates me,
I see
the girl,
my shadow and the sea
now dancing slowly
away from me.

———————————

Mother, grandmother, social worker and liberal hippie from
North Carolina... I found my voice in poetry.
Allpoetry.com/Becki_Friend

[Stephen Harris]

The House Sparrow

not noted for its pleasant song
too common midst the garden throng
not like the finch with gold wing flair
few take the time to see him there

with pit coal face and charcoal chest
and unwashed shirt on off white breast
bad brawlers' eyes with blackened look
too slow to move from fleeting hook

old scaly boots and scabby claws
a well soiled coat of grimy floors
all drab in garb of common throw
is dressed the dullish house sparrow

now I will stop and newly gaze
upon this bird of fleeting days
then sitting down I'll stay a while
And learn from natures gentle style

the waistcoats made of silver down
a jacket tweed of ruddy brown
with specks of tourmalines black fleck
and Whitby jet around his neck

in short sweet tweets this learned mage
who wears grey hair of aging sage
drops crystal drops of love when heard
how lovely is this homely bird?

I am from Wakefield, West Yorkshire and am a train driver by
profession. I came to writing poetry late in life. Largely as a way
to express my feelings, my thoughts and experiences.
Allpoetry.com/Atryst

[Gennaro P. Raso]

My Dying Father's Vision

see her— across the cratered rutted street
standing under the streetlight
glow mingling with the night mist
emanating incandescent golden luminosity

she garbs herself in diaphanous shades of alabaster
like a statuesque remnant
her flaxen hair flows like pale ashen wildflowers clinging on an
undulating vine—
her eyes are bright and soft as a newborn
see her smiling slowly like a grandmother

my body once trembled like the interminable quaver of a
rattlesnake's tale
now still like a planted worn rock winding down like an old clock
no longer the scurry-eyed sentry pacing— waiting for the foe of
the ages to arrive
dart like an alley cat, no, saunter like a giraffe head held high

---

Gennaro P. Raso is from St.Catharines, Ontario. Retired started
writing poetry recently to fill his time. Finds it emotionally
cathartic. Allpoetry.com/Gennaro_P_Raso

[NP Schneider]

I Choose To Destroy Myself

Above the streets,
cars are the wind,
semi-truck tires clash like thunder,
a downpour of rain
crashes on stone brick walls.

Below on the dirt roads,
oak trees fence with leafy foils
& clacking kendo wood.

I hide from the storm,
legs crossed on a cinderblock
under a concrete umbrella,
spongey denim, translucent tee
& the highway over my head.

Underneath the freeway sleeps
moss & brown shattered
gemstone glass—
a beer bottle delight.

Street lights flicker &
reflect in the waterfall,
a daughter of a one day river.
Golden koi fish leap & swim
over street barricades,

a solar flash shimmers
through tear drop rain—
mistaken for a dragon's flame.

Lightning strikes as a strong
silent whisper, an urge to take over.

I came out with needles on my mind,
shoe lace wrapped tight
around blood.

Chipped concrete, spray can
graffiti of skull & crossbones,
unreadable gang names,
wet white paint still dripping names—
names that erase in the rain.

The rain has trapped me
here in this shivering cave.

A cave where fungus grows
on dirt patches alongside
some dandelions & flies
feast on a dead deer.

Fresh roadkill far from home, the forest,
dried here on the dirt underpass,
gunshot holes healed over,
but crows peck at its melted
weeping wax eyes.

Veins are rock the more you poke,
rusted razorblades reflect
coagulated crimson.

Sounds of rushing water
start to dry, the koi fish
flip-flop & kick up dust,
Birds strike the band,
& cicadas echo screams.

My breath turns to fog,
a pearl snowflake floats
down & melts into a puddle—
return to rain.

Icicles freeze overhead,
snowfall blankets the muddy grass,
cryogenic flowers, & tree branches.

Cars crawl on the highway &
steam rises above the asphalt.

Even the dead deer is covered
in a china white grave,
icy skin rests until
thawing in the morning.

Emptiness enfolds a sheer
distance— holding my hand
in a purifying blizzard.

N.P. Schneider is from Brooklyn, New York. I've moved around most of my life and never settled down. Most of my time is spent writing about nature, drug abuse, and suicide. I write to not feel alone. Allpoetry.com/N.P._Schneider

[Randy Gravelle]

Night Woods

Fresh laid mulch cumbersome and raw
trips along trail in gathering darkness maw.

Teenage flippant tenders coins and paper notes
clown hats from comics and newspaper sail boats.

Canines can't resist their warm frothy drool
flapping furious already a disguised cruel

Avocado trees sporting miniature fruits
as dinky as the flower branch's feminine new chutes.

Clustered tightly in a blastula of sorts
that won't multiply but will shrink and fall short

the ebony bark exfoliating dry
green spit deep within the pit tip getting high

Out of reach the lustrous green goddess
dripping drops oily props lower branches modest

Ornamental hard shell waxy grip barely
dropping softly to the sparkling underbelly squarely

In the shady depths underneath where the trunk
swallows hard in meditation lonely servile monk.

Hymns symphonic of Ludwig's deaf ear
the forest and her nuclear family does not hear

Spellbound every sound generated there
penetrate the mist as it hovers lower air.

Critters from lichen to Monarch butterfly
outer layer skeeters dribble bloody sigh.

The mulch now soft baked from sunshine glare and heat
salad bar for near and far emerging there to eat.

No curtains, blinds, isinglass shades
moons cast owl blast streaming light brigades

penetration undulation solitude in sound
a warbler branch lit upon snaps and hits the ground.

Silence broken a minuscule bird
dazed in the mulch only one that heard.

Mr Moon under layers peering at the woods
tries to sell himself as cheese and other spacely goods

mosquitos wrap and tuck their straws away to sleep
springy singing frogs cacophonously peep

The woodsy branches grasses and still air
serve as blankets, pillows covers dusty ruffles for all there.

Randy lives in Los Angeles with his partner of 17 years and their 2 JRT's. Among his publications: the Los Angeles Times, and won 1st place in summer 2020 "Dreamers" poetry contest. Allpoetry.com/joebrazeau

[Raymond Fenech Gonzi]
The Glory and the Dreams

The ground upon which I walk
is alien to me and the century I lived in
too young with a different mentality.
I've paced this ground as if there was a mist
from my waist down and I couldn't see my feet,
nor where each step fell and what lied beneath.
I've continuously hoped I was in a nightmare,
that eventually would all come to an end
with a sudden waking to a fanfare of reality;
my eyes would behold verity as I imagined it to be.
Only half of my body and spirit are here
the rest of my being is beyond, aloof and alert,
in another time warp where innocence was bliss
and children still believed in fairy tales.

I've walked this earth thinking I could make a change
but I tripped over one delusion after another;
human values and kindness wiped clear,
love was all make-belief, castles in the air;
mistresses came and went without any remorse
and I was left grieving out in the cold,
to contemplate where I had gone wrong;
until I believed there was no heaven nor a God.
It was a time I realized 'the end' came all too often
and in real life no one lives "happily ever after."
All I see reminds me of something that is gone

into the abyss we try not to speak about:
humans design their own dreams and glory
but when they succumb to the angel of death,
where are their dreams, where is the glory?

Raymond Fenech Gonzi PhD embarked on his writing career as a journalist at 17. Twice nominated for The Pushcart Prize he is a writer, poet, editor and publisher.
Allpoetry.com/Raymond_Fenech_Gonzi

[Shanon Marie Norman]

Try, Try, Triolet (When Cartwheels Fail)

Your idiot voice is a nagging echo between my ears.
The antagonistic provocations shove my soul.
"Take some Risks!" and "Foolish plans!" irk like fears --
Your idiot voice is a nagging echo between my ears.

I thought you'd finally accept me after all these years,
but to you no age I ever turn will be considered old.
Your idiot voice is a nagging echo between my ears.
The antagonistic provocations shove my soul.

I went the distance to end up back at square one.
You rained on my parade after we made a float.
You laughed when I melted under your exalted sun.
I went the distance to end up back at square one.

When I had strength and courage, I had some fun -
but you shot me down just to get my goat.
I went the distance to end up back at square one.
You rained on my parade after we made a float.

Risks like cartwheels and tickets were explored.
Nerve damage and hysteria were the results.
Why can't you let me be boring and bored?
Risks like cartwheels and tickets were explored.

Some of you say I fall upon my sword ---
Yet my adult cult can handle any insult.
Risks like cartwheels and tickets were explored.
Nerve damage and hysteria were the results.

A Rare Stake Well Done or Sanctuary Seeker could be good titles
for the Autobiography, although I doubt I'll ever get that book
finished. I'm an ordinary hero who enjoys writing and reading.
Allpoetry.com/White_Sissy

[Mister Colvet]

crystal surfaces

slouching
with glazed hammed eyeballs
staring at pink bits of flesh
cutting the grapefruit
along the improper axis again
passing rubbing fingertips
over crystal surfaces

plasma surges
through ancient crystal lattices
clicking clockwork spins of metal flanges
pressurizing
the sac of air hanging over your head
popping blood balloons
in the children's section of the library

but wetness makes paper get damp
and salt curls the ends of your hair
sleeping in a mountain of fluff
traversing slopes of translucent mirrors
with skate blades
writing cursive in hardened blue
panes of glass
tethered with crazy glue
while the dimple in your chest caves in
pushing on the swallowed globs of guilt

kitchenware put in the tumbler upside down
squirming into your skin
like hedgehog needles
keep the wrist moving
as your drag your hand across the page
sweeping feet
in dragging streaks of synchronicity
since flailing limbs
never break the fall on icy sidewalks
and names written in marker on picnic tables
fade in the sun
since whiskey runs dry
at the end of the trail

lacking backup batteries
for your handheld flashlight
no more Cheyenne pepper juice
for your wand of protection
do deer still tense in headlights?
or do they signal go
like stationary green orbs?
the clouds will clear
when the sky rolls
its ball of light down the hillside
getting it stuck
over the fence of the neighbor's yard

glass shattering with bronze tubes
reverberating chugging lulls
your foot's the first thing to turn blue

extremities are so finnicky and reliant
with stringing bits of pink flesh
only hidden
under grooved sheets of germs
blanketed
under pillars of sloughing cell bodies

in amazement and amusement
by the commonality of household wares
as you curl into your crocheted blanket
watching the windows for a signal
that the punishment
and abuse of the sun is over
into the healing remedy of moonlight

as I suckle on honey drops
and rub my fingers over crystal surfaces
latticed and interwoven for eternity
in containers
of granulated epsom salts

A plain-clothes engineer, writer, artist, and general over-thinker
wrapped into one epithelial sheet deemed human.

I have coined the theme of my work as 'Bio-organic surrealism'.
Allpoetry.com/Colvet

[Bobbie Breden]

Greening Goddess Gaia

Behold the forest empress, deep, dark, quiet, cool,
home of towering pine and lowly toadstool

Observe here the countryside consort, flower covered meadow
refuge to rabbit, butterfly, bird, and timid brown doe

Regard, I am the jungle's ruler, growing fierce and free,
fearsome and tropical, with chaotic purpose and intensity

Survey me, the landscape's queen, serene green scene
with parterres, gardens, and groves haven to the oscine passerine

Contemplate quietly the mountain monarch, rolling foothill
verdant valley, rushing river, brook, creek, stream, and water mill

I, the greening's sovereign, tangled hedgerow, aspen thicket,
maple copse
blackberry bramble, twining honeysuckle vine, towering treetops

I am Gaia, ancestral earth-mother, goddess divine
I am the embodiment of nature, and this terrestrial sphere is my
shrine

Retired Lady Leatherneck (US Marine), Renaissance woman, and a lover of life's mysteries. I'm interested in how others view the universe, and welcome opportunities to see it through their eyes. Allpoetry.com/Captain_B2

[L S Austin]

Saint Edmund's Town

Steam plumes pinpoint this town's position.
Modernity shadows ancient tracks.
Silos, grey below a wintry sky.
Liberty and law, born here by pact.

Crowded narrow streets in grid-like form
Guide footsteps toward its ardent core.
Uphill to the busy market square,
Then down to the silent Abbey wall.

Saint Edmund's shrine, a cloistered corner.
Potent Abbey. Sanctuary sought.
Overawed the ancient settlement,
The centre of prayer and pious thought.

Naked rubble columns soar aloft
Stand guard as powerful Abbots sleep.
Witness to history's lengthy role;
Timeless secrets they silently keep.

Pungent aroma from copper vats
Passes over the old Vineyards hill.
The ancient craft, palette perfected;
Beer, pumped though pubs till pint glasses fill.

Time-seared shop fronts line central streets,
Traditional windows, glazed of old.
Wares for sale, lit by glass bulbs,
Entice the moneyed in from the cold.

Ancient twin-gable, stone edifice
Stands, watchful over all market days.
Centuries pass, with purpose new,
It's facade untouched; an unchanged gaze.

I am from East Anglia, UK. I currently live in Suffolk with my
husband and dog. I write poetry from my inspiration, wherever it
takes me. Allpoetry.com/Rosesapling28

[Robert Poleski]

Remembering Old Home

retracing my steps through back home-
the old house I was born
first love
neighbor's daughter
the old oak tree-
still remembers kisses in its shade
melancholy veil embraces thoughts
roots abandoned in the barren soil
dying- cut out from the nourishing breath

moments snatched from my grasp
the walls that witnessed my secrets
still echo with bittersweet memories-
left it all
to discover new horizons

a mirage looms on the silver brim of history
from the Land on the Vistula
a thriving empire stretched from the Baltic to the Black Sea
under the Jagiellonian Kings
the phantoms glide
by the windows of my mind
speaking a strange native tongue
make mind misty
eyes moist
languid gloom chases off starry spheres

wolf's-bane roots
tangle and snare the heartbeat
wet melancholic darkness
bangs on the roof of the creed

ghosts of Mickiewicz
who knew that the heart can burn what the mind cannot break
"I was there indeed, drank the wine and the mead,
What I saw and heard wrote here for all you to read"

the place where Copernicus moved Earth
at the center of the universe
where Chopin left his heart
created the new world with his music
Sobieski beat the Turks at the gates of Vienna

as Coleridge Keats and Hunt sung
"Till love and fame to nothingness do sink...
never have relish
in the faery power of
unreflecting love"
Kosciusko's freedom fighting blood
sunk in Polish and American lands

the native land of John Paul II
"The future starts today, not tomorrow...
have no fear of moving into the unknown"--
a prophecy of the incoming storms

so I left all--
not content with living a harrowing life
left the country of my youth
to discover new horizons
herald the new dawn--
snatched by the omnipotent
never benevolent time

What I see is my own world, my whole intimate universe, with
my mind, my heart, looking inside things, inside feelings, what
makes it laugh or cry, love or hate, what makes it feel pleasure or
pain. Allpoetry.com/Robert_Poleski

[William La Civita]

Snowdrops

Verdant blades and phallic buds
push through the frozen earth
toward the lean sun of winter.
The mulch is scarcely frosted
when the sepals part and the blossoms nod,
revealing petals and a green-tipped bell —
Spring seems so near, we cheer,
neglecting nature's caution.

A nor'easter off the coast attacks,
the blizzards onslaught—
snow, sleet, rain.
Its piles swell with slush and ice,
then twilight's arctic air solidifies the glaze.

Between white drifts,
the clods are bare,
snowdrops surprise!
For days they thrive,
now hundreds pop,
resilience blooms
in this flinty clime.

———————————————

Retired, gay, married, working-class: I have been writing poetry
for years, but I not displayed it until now. My influences are
William Carlos Williams, Kenneth Rexroth, and Emily Dickerson
etc. Allpoetry.com/Blll

[Gennaro P. Raso]

Frozen Out In February

honking car horns clanging street cars roaring buses herald a new
day born

stiff, crawling like an infant from my glazed appliance stenciled
cardboard tomb grimacing slowly at the day that looms

from rusted subway bars rises noxious eye watering face twisting
heated air, I hide my paper room and take my place there

crouched like a tiny gnome sinking in the frigid wet brown snow,
February's laughing gusts gnaw at my stooped body with another
chilling blow

purple face and gritty crooked fingers exposed dirt-stained toes,
temperature quickly drops ache inside me quickly grows

curl my shivering smelly grime crusted body into a compact heat
ball pulling tight my tattered spattered coat and moth-eaten shawl

like chilly mist floating down the street the obituary travelled;
toothless Joe died last night
contorted body locked in an embrace, blistered ash grey face stuck
to the metal pole of a streetlight

eight short hours of warmth to savor the day's sunlight made
more precious by gelid night

only the second month live one more day, warmth birth and
blooms wait one more day when warmth resumes

Gennaro P. Raso is from St.Catharines, Ontario. Retired started
writing poetry recently to fill his time. Finds it emotionally
cathartic. Allpoetry.com/Gennaro_P_Raso

[Nancy Jackson]

To the One who Hears My Pleas

I reclined beside the ocean's edge and
stared blearily towards the horizon.
Waves curled and twisted
and washed over rocks and sand,
churning sea-caps into frothy air
before retreating to dance anew.

I drifted into a trance.

Barely aware of the shards in my feet
I blithely skipped across
white-ribboned waves
which slumped and crashed
into the jagged cliff faces.

And without warning, steel-trap jaws and
needlepoint-sharp teeth
rose from under ice-capped peaks
and clamped down tightly around my legs.
I was pulled under again and again.

My head bobbed above the waterline
as I squinted into the misty haze,
but my foe eluded me.
Then I heard a wailing noise so piercing,

so guttural and anguished, that I ached even more
to flee the beast below.

Searing pain pulsed within me
as I watched sticky crimson droplets splay over
the sea-foam green of the ocean.
The frenzied beast had gnawed me in two,
and the heartrending sound wafting in the air
was rising from deep within me.

Startled awake, I searched for blood, ready to die.

An inexpressible agony pierced my frame.
And with temples throbbing
and breathing labored
I raised my head and my hands
and cried out with unconsolable explosions
to the One who hears my pleas.

My brother is dead.

Nancy Jackson grew up on a Virginia peninsula surrounded by
the ocean, rivers, and creeks. She developed an affinity for the
mountains during college. Both settings continue to influence her
poetry. Allpoetry.com/Nancy_daisygirl

[Robert Poleski]

Four Seasons - Rain Symphony

I. Intermezzo

it begins
a whispering in the air echoes through the silence of trees in the
audience   tinkling sound
as the first pearls of rain drop onto the water lustre
Chopin's Raindrop Prelude
instruments tuning
each droplet
an instrument in the orchestra
the sound like a glassy clinking of
champagne flutes
lilting and clear
sound intensifies
   huffing wind crescendo   .

for the sheet of the rain nears

II. Spring drizzle

spring misty rain falls down
frail as a Scottish smirr
sinless and glistening
raindrops fall
wiping off the night's stillness
foggy dew like a warm butter melting on the face

the melancholic cry of a lonely fox echoes
    through the silence of the trees
Debussy
Jardins sous la pluie
violin's dark timbre in the clouds weeping

teardrops from the sky

III. Summer rain

summer rain descends in the gleam of silver drops
sparkly and effervescent
bubbles hit the skin
the wall of cool refreshment
the huffing wind rises up
stirs the leaves
the rove of rain on the roof
full of ghosts
tap and sigh upon the window glass
as they listen for the reply
droplets fall in a rhythm
become the song
phut-phut-phut like the ripened nuts
hitting the ground
ball-bearings beat the rooftops
Vivaldi baroque concerto-
watch out for the thunderstorms

go dance in the rain
with clouds at your heels

IV. Autumn storms

autumn skies are vengeful
shrouds of clouds coil and writhe
race across the sky thrumming
with the charged energy
desperate to release
the rain sissing and hissing
teeming onto the spongy earth
caterwauling sound fills the air
    Beethoven's Pastoral
the wind whips up into a frenzy
shrieking omen of the carnage to follow
starts with big sopping drops of moisture
wild and indiscriminate
plump missiles of mass destruction
splattering onto the soft soil
then a cacophony of sounds follow

the conductor
loses control of his orchestra

V. Winter deluge

winter sky is the widow's tomb
bedarkened and weeping
the crabbed kraken-cruel clouds
cough out great gouts of water
balloons of the sopping moisture
Noah's-Ark cataclysm pouring down

in a biblical deluge
the unending cataract of water sluices from the sky
the gutters stream like the tumbling waterfalls
don't dare go out close the heavens' gate

grab the snuzzy blanket
pour the glass of wine by your fireplace
stare in someone's warm eyes-
hear some quiv'ring and tremble in the Purcell's baroque songs

———————

What I see is my own world, my whole intimate universe, with
my mind, my heart, looking inside things, inside feelings, what
makes it laugh or cry, love or hate, what makes it feel pleasure or
pain. Allpoetry.com/Robert_Poleski

[Alwyn Barddylbach]

Nature Comes to Those Who Wait

Idle wings a poem sow
till the landscape makes me yearn,
your brush spills well above my plough,
how the heavy clay must turn.

Clothe the turf beneath me burning,
ancient oak now shed their skin,
young sapling press my brow discerning,
trim the borders sleek and thin.

Wintry fields in state of mourning,
my weathered brambly creek innate,
downstream the bed and furrows stony,
trick the banshee break the slate.

These hills inspire the onward journey,
nature comes to those who wait.

———————————

Celebrating one of nature's most colourful advocates, Vincent van
Gogh whom she so richly rewarded in his humble work, vivid
imagination and patience, a sonnet - AB Blue Mountains
Allpoetry.com/Barddylbach

[Laura Sanders]

The Scottish Highlands

In Scotland, the mountains rise up - tall giants of the land,
looming and dominating the wild, pink gorse uplands.
Sheltering the lively leaping salmon laden rivers,
looking like grey snakes, across landscapes they slither.

The land is steeped in history, shaped by its geography.
The clans once roamed here, wild, brave and free.
Ancient Caledonian forests cover pockets of this place.
Pine trees and evergreen shrubs have been cut down in haste...

but saplings have been planted in age old turf,
where the Scottish wild cat, a shy creature lurks
and here the red squirrel scampers and ptarmigan roam.
Mountains, rivers, lochs, animals, make Scotland a beautiful
home.

I live in a beautiful part of England and I receive inspiration for
writing my poems , simply by walking and observing the
countryside throughout the year. I also enjoy observing people
and nature.
Allpoetry.com/Laura_Sanders

[Stephen Harris]

Me and my Grandfather

often deeds done will draw me to visions
thoughts that are but glaciers, frozen memories
that now with age far outnumber dreams
like when I take the cloth to clean my spectacles
and slowly demist each lens from the fingers fog
with the calm purpose of the philosopher
who sits and ponders over pools of thought

it is times like these that I remember my grandfather
seated with his pint pot of tea
steeped and stewed to a tar liquorish brown
the cryptic newspaper held open to crease
margins scrawled with unintelligible glyphs
and his well-worn pencil pincered and poised

all this I see while by his side
always by his side it seemed
watching him and his cigarette
as it danced that singular dance of swirling ribbons
till it ascended to the yellow stained Gods
and then cried from the heights in prophetic plea
his frail blackening lungs silent, dumb
until the day he breathed as if through a straw

sometimes he visits me still and I see him clearly in the mirror
his young lock of hair combed and cut for marriage

and his kind wise eyes looking back at me
from days now as dead as him
but yet we both smile
though I grieve and am lost in the depth of longing

I am from Wakefield in the North of England and am 52 years of age. I am beginning to write a few more poems that are autobiographical in essence. I hope you enjoy.
Allpoetry.com/Atryst

[Stephen Hollins]

Golden Fruit

Spanish-orange candles flicker
against a yellow fish-shaped vase
two glasses of red wine stand empty
as do I, ransacked after the storm
collapsed, fallen
I have been dragged to the other side, again
tendrils in her spider web provoke me to fight
to cross over to the sticky side
where I become a torched shadow of myself
ambushed, chest open to black widow's claws
fighting, frenzied, fatigued
the sacred cord that binds us severed

enter the robber
creeping into a battlefield fog
his Dickensian fingers pickpocket our hallowed ring
that tribute of gold our entwined heartbeats
weaved together for future dreams
nurtured in the soil of frank-heartedness

enter the policeman
with a black rubber truncheon hitting our heads
throwing our band of faith into oblivion
'Oi none of you can have it
I'm out of here, I won't be coming back.'

enter the nurse
running to peg garden stakes
that winter winds have blown down
she hangs up vines for new fruit
to smile in sun and swing the amber moon breeze
not to rot in dark poisoned earth
bursting out a martyr's bloodshot eye

enter the tailor vagabond
he holds my sunrise shoulders
turning my grey hands
green
to ripen the golden fruit

I live on beautiful Waiheke Island in New Zealand. I specialize in
Improv for theatre, dance, clown, mime, teaching adults to
become more playful, building and renovation.
Allpoetry.com/Stephen_Hollins

[Brittney Mills]
Tecate

We zoom through the hillside
Nine of us are stuffed in a dirty van
My sweaty shirt sticks to my back
as I gaze out at the colorful blur
Shanties are a never-ending string
of pink, green, yellow, brown
Some are just plain cardboard
and I'm humbly grateful for
but somewhat ashamed of
my comforts back home

We take a gravel road to the left
that leads to a ranch with no address
with a large metal fence and gate
and pretty pink and white flowers
Chickens are out pecking the yard
The ranch was built using loan money
from American banks but never repaid
because they moved back to Mexico
and then built a house so they
wouldn't have to live in a shanty

B. Mills lives in TN with her family. She began writing in 2005 and graduated Cum Laude from Jackson State CC with an Associate Degree in 2015 and was also in the PTK honor society. Allpoetry.com/B._Mills

[Ally Marcella]

Forest

We camped in the woods under the stars
pitched six tents, we stood and admired
our handiwork, took photos for our memoirs,
then fixed dinner and drinks before we retired

In the moonlight, a lone silhouette of a wolf
his howl was interrupted by a distant shriek
the wolf froze, then bolts into the night
a breeze brought a chill and goosebumps

We zipped ourselves in, shaken with a jolt
as gossamer hands with fingers of fog creeps in slyly
and searches, breathes within the shadows of trees
arms extend, reaches out, and glides by blithely

A black hooded figure arrives, its transparent robe
drags along the ground, it shrieks loudly
We watch it float back into the forest,
from whence it came

———————————

Ally Marcella is from Southern California. She thinks of new poems while hand quilting. And likes taking long walks during the evening with her two dogs. Allpoetry.com/Ally_Marcella

[Marcy Clark]

You Can't Always Get What You Want

The Doctor exhales a hymn
and eyes blur behind newspapers read every day by her bedside

He weeps when the tests do not lie
and early October he loses her
leaving him and their threadbare Yorkie to grieve

He and the dog limp through the end of the year
until, with a soft sigh, the dog departs on a rainy January morning
and he is left with his rosary

Scattered souvenirs tarnish him
he waits his turn
and when breath does not cease he uproots his unraveled life

tucks, in the front seat of the Ranger,
a map cascading billows of mountain peaks
and acres of timber between him and the clouds

and in the back seat
a footlocker guarding his loaded Smith and Wesson,
his wife's hand knit sweater, her ashes mixed with the boys'
and slips away

In a hollow swathed in silence
the cabin slumbers ten switchback forest miles
from the nearest whistle stop

a place where he can be done with the world
on his own terms

He sleeps a fifteen hour day
and at dusk folds pictures of his family into his jacket pocket

hoists his weapon with a steady hand
and shoulders past a squalling screen door

The last of winter stings his cheeks
and his pulse skips beneath the full moon
the gun crooning at his side

A starving calico explodes from the shadows
and slams its withered poem against his legs

The gun falls silent beneath each stanza
and he places it on the stoop
to crochet the cat's bony silhouette in his embrace

and hears his wife and children whispering from the forest
as he carries her inside

Writing poetry has become my passion, my time machine-fueled
with both sad and wonderful memories that keep my loved ones
near. Allpoetry.com/Grandmakittyfl

[Keith Pailthorp]

What Is a Man?

at mid-morning Vlady arose from his desk
entered his marble bathroom
dropped his trousers and silk undies
and deposited two perfectly-tapered turds in the gilded toilet
let history note, neither sank and both stank
afterward he wiped not forward but backward
as Mamochka had urged
he hefted his shorts and pants
surveying his creation, he reluctantly flushed
he washed his hands
an ablution to Mamochka
refreshed, Vlady returned to his desk
to order the slaughter of more Ukrainian children

Keith Pailthorp a retired state bureaucrat living in Davis,
California on a contrived pond and working on an unauthorized
autobiography of his checkered past.
Allpoetry.com/Keith_Pailthorp

[Alwyn Barddylbach]

Mortal Rose

My mortal sap was in the softness of
the soils that freed my morbid sanguine vein
and filled me with desire to catch the light.

My sleek lips charred like bitter cocoa seed
in midday lingered; drops of dew hung down
my cheek on prickly thorns of sufferance.

Fragrance of night in a sultan's palace,
prayer to the moon for visible solace,
child of the half-light, serenity's deed.

I who wear the sun surrender this hour,
nightingale in shadows doubtful sung;
cast not your dark blanket of cult or need,
arcane myth, script in scorn, culpable creed
- on me -

La vie du soleil, nothing lives for ever.

A true black rose has not been found in nature, a tragic romance,
mortal like any other. Nature refutes man, voice of the rose, blank
sonnet - AB Blue Mountains Allpoetry.com/Barddylbach

[Margaret Harrison]

My Dad's Garden

My dad's garden had plenty vegetables.
Dad grew so much on a large piece of land
there were so many from garden to table
Corn stalks grew high in a row
and pull back the husk the corn was yellow.
so it was fun eating kernels from corn on the cob
Dad working in the garden was a hard job
Tomatoes in a row
pick them when they are red.
if they were green, Dad's answer was no.
We had lettuce that you can pick
when leafy green instead.
Radishes pull the green stems out of the ground.
Radishes are bright pink and white inside
that is what I found.
We had carrots pick them before eaten by the rabbits.
We pull the green stems up just like a radish.
We had snowpeas and opened up the pod.
We could eat them without a nod.
Dad always said "yes"
Dad had a plan
Where to plant the garden.
What to plant in the garden.
I used to play with the beehive made in a log
the bee buzzed before it stung me
The log was part of the garden.

I am from Bergen County in New Jersey I started writing poetry in eighth grade. I am a proud Aunt of Many nieces and Nephew and now I am a Great Aunt .

I am the fifth child of seven children Allpoetry.com/Violinstrings

[Stephen Hollins]

waiting for a helicopter

on a glass balcony
admiring sparkling Oneroa Bay
dotted with anchored sailboats
colored canvas on turquoise waters

a few light watercolor clouds hang over the sea
at the beach, tiny bodies float and splash
people and cicadas abuzz
in this sunshine vacationers landscape
Christian Dior's Poison perfume wafts by
green hedges, molding architecture, walkways
Thai flavored chicken, mushrooms
peppers, cashew nuts, coriander
and steaming rice
water my nostrils
in my left hand a black Monteith's beer

the inside world of my dogged headphones
paints dark, nebulous colors
the drone of black music
in the trees
a gallows noose hangs
with my name on it
a thin glass wall separates me from this paradise
skin itches, backaches, feet on fire
inside shoes, I cannot remove

lovers have erased me
they drink and laugh
it is me that has put myself here
and swallowed the key
beyond the veil of paradise

_____

I live on beautiful Waiheke Island in New Zealand. I specialize in Improv for theatre, dance, clown, mime, teaching adults to become more playful, building and renovation.
Allpoetry.com/Stephen_Hollins

[Terence O'Leary]

Lost Love Deliria

AWAKENING

Sleep and slumber, dreams of wonder... weaving,
morning's vacuum broke the spell
Pitted pillow, note of parting... cleaving,
"from your friend, a fond farewell"
Sunrise throbbing, twilight aching... grieving,
daydreams, flashbacks, nightmares knell
Pale phantasms, visions sneaking... thieving,
plot to fill the empty shell

12 DELIRIA

1st Delirium: Collapses
Fractured sky bolts, billows bursting... rumbling,
heavens tighten, turn the vise
Horsemen saddle shafts of lightning... stumbling,
jagged highways must suffice
Ruptured welkin, hailstones cracking... crumbling,
ocean basements choked with ice
Toxic tongues in whispers stinging... mumbling,
washed out laughter pays the price
Thunder drumming, droplets muzzled... tumbling,
naked pearls of paradise
Burning passions, cinders smoking... humbling,
ashes shaped in sacrifice

2nd Delirium: Descents
Asphalt alleys, ashen faces... frowning,
blowing bubbles, chewing gum
Drinking ale from tavern tankards... downing,
moonlit beads of painted rum
Stony stars and sea misshapen... drowning,
humble rivers' rhythms hum
Apparitions aspirating... clowning,
diamonds dying, minstrels strum
Incandescent candles conquered... crowning,
vacant vapours, cold and numb

3rd Delirium: Fates
Tempest turmoil, tapered turrets... holding,
dungeons, dragons, chains and racks
Wheels of fortune, Tarot temptress... molding,
Hangmen, Towers, One Eyed Jacks
Sand dune castles, cryptic candles... folding,
warping walls of liquid wax
Idols colder, combed and coddled... scolding,
hide in fissures, peek through cracks

4th Delirium: Lost Souls
Sunken cities, pilgrims peering... gawking,
squinting eyeballs, blazing sun
Janus facing, shepherds chasing... stalking,
friends embrace before they shun
Tearooms steaming, tumult teeming... talking,
lovers listen, poets pun
Broken stones unanchored, quaking... rocking,

slipping, falling, one by one
Beaten pathways, footsteps marking... mocking,
wedged in webs which spiders spun
Circus shelters, big tops tumbling... locking,
people pacing, soon they're none
Numbered exits, zeros numbing... knocking,
midnight daylight's days undone
Moon blood shackles, shivers shaming... shocking,
starlight striders streaking, stun
Hushed but harried hermits waiting... walking,
restless rainbows on the run
Pixies, elves, and echoes bouncing... balking,
fading fast when dawn's begun
Bantum butterflies are flitting... flocking
sometimes conquered, overrun
Hocus pokus, seers focus... squawking,
voodoo wavered, witchcraft won

5th Delirium: Introspection
Sundown furnace, fires fading... coughing,
dusky dew drops drain the air
Empty chalice, sipped in silence... quaffing,
thirsting shadows unaware
Looking glass and lattice scorning... scoffing,
local loser gapes and stares
Faces covered, dancing naked... doffing,
peering inside, hope despairs

6th Delirium: The Void
Tales of taboos, mystic mythos... missing,

windows shuttered, bolted door
Kindled candles, tongues and anvils... hissing,
heavy hammers, echoes roar
Dark deceivers, raven charmers... kissing,
dragging demons from the shore
Hopeless hollows filled with doubters... dissing
standing empty - nevermore

7th Delirium: Searching
Martyred monks haunt runic ruins... feting,
banging broken bells below
Vaulted hallways, voided voices... grating,
echo Chinese chimes aglow
Granite graveyards, specters spooking... mating,
blackened bushes, roses grow
Mutant dwarfs seek midget migrants... waiting,
veiled in vacuum, ice and snow

8th Delirium: Nighttime
Throbbing drumheads, fingers blazing... steaming,
coins of copper, beggar's plea
Rusty residues of resin... streaming,
opal amber filigree
Orphan shades in shallow shadows... teeming,
steeping twigs in twilight tea
Cloister doorsteps, Prophet's gaming... scheming,
tracing tracks of destiny
Blacksmiths blanching, horseshoes glowing... gleaming,
partially sheathed in black debris

Phantoms feigning, nightmares scathing... screaming,
dusty dreamers drifting free

9th Delirium: Emptiness
Water wheels in wastelands... turning,
drowning relics in the slum
Rumpled rags of fashioned burlap... burning,
lit by bandits blind and dumb
Pastured prisons, ponies bridled... yearning,
forest fairies under thumb
Sounds inside of cauldrons coughing... churning,
blaring bugles, tattooed drum

10th Delirium: Alienation
Rain unravelling, wistfully weeping... falling,
treacle trickling, fickle sky
Mushrooms sprinkled, visions sprouting... sprawling,
seagulls drowning, dolphins die
Rabble gasping, spirits broken... crawling,
lonely lonesome swallows cry
Babbling brooks and breakers ebbing... bawling
puppies paddle, puppets sigh
People passing ripple past me... calling,
rainbow colours, collars high
Chaos seething, lepers looting... stalling,
stealing stallions on the sly
Pencils pausing, scholars scrambling... scrawling,
scratching scribbles, asking why

11th Delirium: Jetsam
Silver sails sway pallid pirates... prowling,
Jolly Rogers, wind and sound
Parrots perching, tattered feathers... fouling,
tethered talons, tied and bound
Shipwrecked foghorns, trumpets stranded... howling,
spiral springs of time unwound
Magic moonlight, shimmers shaking... scowling,
burnt out matchsticks washed aground
Prairie wolfs, coyotes calling... yowling,
witching hours, midnight hounds
Tightrope walkers, grizzlies grunting... growling,
seeking islands, lost and found

12th Delirium: Relief
Slumber shattered, vapours captive... haunting,
chained in mirrors, breaking free
Scarlet skylines, daylight dawning... daunting,
rivers rushing to the sea
Silence softens, sandmen whisper... wanting,
piercing rafters, turning keys
Shadows shudder, notions fluster... flaunting,
moonbeam bullets meant for me
Mind in migraine, meadows trembling... taunting,
sparrows speak in harmony

REAWAKENING

Pitter patter, teardrops paling... pearling,
salting scarves in secret drawers

Mist amongst us, smoke rings rising... curling,
climbing from the ocean floors
See-saw circles, senses swerving... swirling,
swept away with silver oars
Courtyard jesters, sceptres twisting... twirling,
push the past to foreign shores
Passing pangs of passions heaving... hurling,
burning bridges, closing doors
Roses wither, icons waning... whirling,
time decays and time restores

Retired, Terrance enjoys sitting in the garden with some tea and a
piece of pie thinking about the word and life and all that, trying to
get inspired. Allpoetry.com/loquaciousicity

[Jesse Fenix]

a black cat

a cat strolls in shades of night
amidst a rain of teeth
jumping over blood puddles
eyes flicker like hungry neon signs
knives wrapped in velvet
play lethal street staccato

mice climb through walls
cemented with lies
then dance with tomorrow's expectation
before slipping under a veil of city fog

_____

Jesse Fenix aka Just Poppy is from Massachusetts and enjoys music, horror movies, zebra finches and writing poetry. Allpoetry.com/Just_Poppy

[Paula Gliot]

Faded Blue Ribbons

paper holding memories
in a woodland refuge set along a tranquil lake abandoned long ago
where children played and grownups dreamed
magic realized in fireflies and campfire tales
stands in the clearing
dwarfed by evergreens and birch trees
beckons you forward to open the door

inside a table covered in years of dust and grime
chairs disheveled, all tousled round
rusted old stove pipe hangs precariously from the ceiling
broken plates and porcelain cups on damaged shelves
wait for the next meal as they have for years
windowsills rotted and blackened by time
shattered glass strewn across wooden floors

against the west wall a hearth proudly stands
once crackling with fresh kindling
a centerpiece of this little cabin home
each stone selected and arranged lovingly
complete with sprawling mantel where cherished items were
displayed
now stands cold, no fire ablaze
no welcoming warmth to share

a small side room hides rusted bed frames
mattresses torn by wood mice seeking shelter from the elements
stacks of books toppled over by years of abandonment
pages yellowed and bindings torn

a bureau leans against a wall
drawers slightly ajar revealing old newspaper lining
one still closed and undisturbed

inside a simple pine box rests
no lock with key keeping contents concealed
beckoning you to reveal what's within
exposing the gems kept secluded all these years
left behind, perhaps overlooked
waiting for the proper time
to uncover the story

inside a lock of hair and broken pocket watch
papers holding memories are bundled up with faded blue ribbons
a testament to those who came before
letters in brittle envelopes whisper to be read
ink faded by years of isolation
left behind to be discovered
revealed to someone who would appreciate their meaning

love letters introduce the residents
courtship sweet and wedding plans
children's birthdays and special triumphs
a lifetime of memoirs kept all these years
secured in this tiny treasure chest
waiting for a chance to live again
reborn in your hands

I live in Palatine, IL. I am a musician, spiritual advisor, and
student of Shamanism. I write because it allows me to express
myself and share my thoughts in a unique medium.
Allpoetry.com/Katdream

[Sarah Marie Reddin]

Raspberry

A sparrow, young, watched the man gently sow the seeds
On a sunday morning, she set her eyes on the evening feed
The Gardener ,only too aware of the sparrow's plot,
Took the scarecrow to the garden next to the orange pot

Day by day she gained courage, moving closer to the tree
While the gardener, armed with a straw broom, was prompting
her to flee
Out he came whistling, to inspect his new found pride
And awaiting behind a wooden fence, the sparrow learned to hide

As the autumn months drew close, the gardener became aware
The tabby from the house next door had lent the bird quite a
scare
Lacking hesitation, he grasped his broom once more
With one swift swing he sent the cat into his neighbours door

Locking eyes with the young sparrow, as if hypnotised
The gardener removed the scarecrow and retreated back inside
Through the kitchen window he could hear the bird sing
And up to the windowsill, the berries she would bring

Languages incompatible,
But the conclusion that would arise
Without the disgruntled gardener
She would not be alive

I am an Irish poet who has been writing for many years . Starting in my own childhood my poems are now shared with my husband and daughter . A coping mechanism and my favourite form of self expression Allpoetry.com/SarahOkeeffe

[Randall Reedy]

Like a Phoenix, Detroit Will Rise

there's a hole in the roof
where robins once nested
their rhythmic tones used to flow
through the joists, and beams
with a bluesy undertone.

that was Detroit, then...

its rundown, beated, abused
rotting in the sunless sky, rain pouring
phantoms used to sing mournful tunes
now they refuse to hum a single note
the only music heard is that of a humming bird

sirens wail like a banshee,
as the serpent slithers out of the dank cupboards,
his eyes become slits in the sun
as the blue skies wave good bye
then the fury of the storm comes

this house stands barren, abandoned, shunned
phantoms and humming birds no longer hum
banished, but still shines with hope
like setting of the sun...as does Detriot

rising from the ashes like a Phoenix

Papa Terminus is from Clinton Townshop MI. A suburb of
Detriot, I have seen first hand the sadness of rundown houses,
and those that were once full of laughter, and passion
Allpoetry.com/Papa_Terminus

[Hivsk Tksvi]

The Gifts That Keep On Taking

Jackals, wolves and coyotes
Chewing and gnawing
In mass entanglement
Of red, foaming teeth
And bleeding tongues
Embroiled with
Infernal, breathless
Rock-cat screaming
Packaged prettily
In twinkling, topaz tissue paper
Tied up with red twine

Bees, wasps and ants
Crawling and stinging
In furious greed
Seeking mass exodus
With needling feet
Emboldened by
Feeble, listless
Baby-bird thrashings
Bound beautifully
In bespeckled, bone-white boxes
Secured with simplistic sinew

Pronounced 'Hawsk Tuk-swa'. I am Midwest born. Poetry has &
continues to be an acceptable outlet for many of the things that
take up residence in my mind & what may or may not be
considered a 'soul'. Allpoetry.com/Hawsk

[Lisa F. Raines]

Abundant skies

as the sunset stretches
across the horizon
thinly swept cirrus streams
herald heavily brooding
snow clouds

purple, gold, and orange
glow in stark contrast to the
growing grey cumulus gloom
borne by the darkening sky

even as these expectant skies
begin to bury us in a
blizzard of wet snow
we will welcome the birth
of a shiny new day

AlisRamie is from North Carolina, USA.
Interests include: philosophy, history, international relations,
poetry, art, design, jazz, funk rock, and some good old soul.
Allpoetry.com/AlisRamie

[William La Civita]

Woodchuck

out of her burrow
assaying skeletal land
crocuses gasping

sleek-furred and chunky
lingering slumbered refreshed
daffodils fearless

scratching the compost
ransacking offshoots and seeds
scilla's blue smiles

rain kindles shudders
unquenchable banqueter
snapdragons tremble

Retired, gay, married, working-class: I have been writing poetry for years, but I have not displayed it until now. My influences are William Carlos Williams, Kenneth Rexroth, Emily Dickerson, etc. Allpoetry.com/Blll

[David I Mayerhoff]

Moving Beyond the Self

I am glued to the inertia
longing to escape this isolated Gibraltar,
the unchanging territory

I spread my wings
to sail beyond the horizon
I do not know where
but my mind creeps with
legs of impatience
urging me out of the comfort zone

fly
lift off your seat of quicksand
elevate to the air
pulse forward
on wings of imagination
soar to Mount Olympus

let go of past history
out there is where the answers lie
and so there should I go

board games meet chess moves
in the mist of the unknown
my pioneer spirit
parts with the handcuffs of the mind now left behind

the gold medal
already awarded with the euphoria
of forward movement

David I Mayerhoff is an emerging literary writer, established scientific author and a Clinical Professor of Psychiatry. He grew up on Long Island and now resides in New Jersey.
Allpoetry.com/David_Mayerhoff

[Paul Goetzinger]

Sundown on Mountain Meadow

A withering gale descends
Across the blades of grass
The wetland echoes a twilight song
Water stills in Gaia's glass

Merganser assembles his evening feast
The forest light grows dim
Shadow crowds the sandy beach
Beaver dozes in his den

Bat unfolds his runic wings
Waving to faded dusk
Moon pursues withering Mars
Westward, adorned in rust

Ebony cloaks his dimming lodge
Evergreen folds his limbs
A chill falls on mountain fields
Night minstrel sings his hymns

Flickering day, greet the night
Flaxen music fades
Aurora dances a celestial ballet
On evenings star lit stage

Paul Goetzinger is a freelance writer and educator from Des Moines, Washington. He has written articles for magazines and other publications for the past 18 years.
Allpoetry.com/Paul_Goetzinger

[Brjan Jalka]

Guards of Ice

guards of ice
in winters grise

caught mid-thrum
flash frozen hum

frigid perch
'twixt silver birch

till sun can bring
warm leave of spring

Laconic Lancashire lad.
Hunkered in the Highlands.

Of one thing I'm certain,
I'm always uncertain.
At least I think so.
Allpoetry.com/Jalk_a_muse

[Lorrie West]

Turkey time

It is turkey time a beautiful turkey in November
On the table it sits for thanksgiving meal
With all the other dishes to pass like mash potato
Sweet potato salad stuffing gravy corn peas
For that delicious dinner dessert is going to be
Apple pie pumpkin pie and pudding happy
Thanksgiving day

My name is Lorrie Ann McConnell-West I write poetry for fun.
I've been writing for years now started in my twenties. I'm fifty
five years old, and I have three children which have grown. I live
in Michigan. Allpoetry.com/lorrie_west

[Alex Quinones]

The Painter

Ode to the painting man
he sees the world in colorful rainbows
he catches the light from the morning sunrise
the crisp wind flowing in spring
reflections against the winter snow

Ode to the painting man
he hears the travelers call
and moves forward faithfully
against the clouded path ahead

—————————————

I have been writing since I was 16 years old. I do not have any formal training. My primary message is hope, serenity, love, and life. Allpoetry.com/Alex_Quinones

[Howard Manser]

Autumn Panoramas

dry amber spires wave

circling leaves whirlybird wings

shed fall feathers float

Poetry is self-revelation. I am a son, brother, husband, father, veteran, and poet hailing from the historic Golden Isles of Georgia. With words, 'Autumn Panoramas' paints a Monet in a Picasso world. Allpoetry.com/ProseAndCons

[Rebecca Sitton]

The Artist

Light trembles off music notes
landing in her hair, where
treble and bass twinkles and fades,
as bourbon glistens in glasses
clutched with scraped-up knuckles
dressed elegantly
to disguise silvery scars
sketched by petty artists
whose talent could have just as easily
etched a beautiful life
with strokes of summer apple red,
and wisps of sun-warmed green highlights,
blown by a quiet breeze,
and painted with golden smiles.

But her spirit was marble,
cold and smooth,
hacked and hewn,
with anger-flashing chisels
and hammers chipping away
all excesses,
until comfort was forfeit; forget
pleasant expressions
and truncated tenderness
from waspish creators

who could choose, but refuse,
to revive.

So shadow sculptors carve
with left-handed claws
that scrape and screech
until all remnants and semblance
of a life born of ease
lay as debris
at her hazard-hardened feet—
because suffering comes cheap,
but the going price for heroism
is everything.

Yet, despite all her sorrow, she smiled,
for at the hand of her trials,
she was in terrible danger
of becoming herself.

Rebecca is a country girl from Texas who has a passion for horses,
writing, inventing, business, science, Oxford commas, and most
importantly—her family. Allpoetry.com/Becky_Stilwell

[David I Mayerhoff]

From Drip To Empty Splash

The sound reveals itself
morphing into a wave
embedded within the leaves, trees, grass and air
as a living presence amidst the people
given voice with a turn of the tongue
a skit of simple dialogue for the young
and a chorus of tenors
harmonizing in baritone

mirth fills the air
with party-goers young and old
shouting scientific nomenclature
exacting grammar
and the loud colors of costumes

I awake from my Rip Van Winkle
and join the acoustic festival
howling songs and dancing ribald
playing the flute at the county symphony
pulsing the jugular of carotid joy

emptiness overtakes me
like a compass sans pointer
seeking the spark
to juice my core

I cannot put my finger
on what is missing
but I sense the absence
in the wounds not seen
that many drown out with strong drink
and infectious guffaw

David I Mayerhoff is an emerging literary writer, established
scientific author, and a Clinical Professor of Psychiatry. He grew
up on Long Island and now resides in New Jersey.
Allpoetry.com/David_Mayerhoff

[Madhuri Anumula]

A journey of faith

I saw him stand behind the curtain
listening to the whispers around
tapping his feet now and then
nodding his head, clearing the air with his horn

Yes, strength of tomorrow awaits
let go the ego off your hands he neighed
hold me and my coat with care
let's tread our way to the green big gate

Home, I see far away in woods
all branches dense covered and crooked
no light I see in proud axe eyes
let the tears wipe dust of the pride

Hold him and truth with all strength
feet you raise alongside and big strides
gone are the days of darkness and pain
leap ahead and ringing the faith bells

———————————

Madhuri, is a software engineer pursuing academic research in
Bengaluru. She likes penning thoughts about life and different
shades of it. Her pen name is her daughter and son names put
together. Allpoetry.com/Mythri_Arjun

[Mark S. Man]

The Last Breath

Now is not the time to pretend or to lie
we both know that soon you will die...

Let's just say what's on our minds today
It's time to weigh the cost of life, and pay.
It's Judgement Day.

You know you've not got long, and it's time to say goodbye
There's no point upsetting anyone, so please be kind
choose your words carefully for those you leave behind.
You know your time has come, so tell me what's on your mind

*[~I]There's something wrong, I feel it in my bones, it's a slow
shadow, a silent pest. A creeping darkness 'inside' willing me to
rest[~IX]*

Now that you've received the call, it's natural to feel some fear
Be ready, settle your mind, now you know that death is near

*[~I]Having looked deep and hard at my reflection
There's no consolation, I expect no compensation
It's time to embrace my final destination*

*I know I'm on my way and scared to be alone...
accepting of my fate, it's time to atone*

I'm struggling to comprehend that soon I will die
and can't believe it's time to say goodbye
Unanswered questions spin around my head
with no hope of answers before I am dead"[~IX]

[~I]Is this really happening?[~IX]
[~I]Is it chance, or divine intervention?[~IX]
[~I]bad luck or devilish intention?[~IX]

[~I]I wish I could stay, I want to live, for just one more day...
Words can't describe the anticipation of when I'll come to rest...
As far as I know, we get one life, this is not a dry run, this is not a test...
Don't take life too seriously, enjoy it while you have the time, to waste a day is such a crime[~IX]

So ill and in such pain, prolonging this life you've nothing to gain
Nothing to look forward to, no reason to remain.
I told him he had done his bit and so,
perhaps now is the time to just let go

In this moment, while you're in pain but aware of your plight
stop thinking about what you've done wrong or right
You tried so hard, you did your best
There's no need to suffer any longer, just relax, let go and rest
Why struggle through another night
It's time to accept you've lost this fight

It's impossible to comprehend
the quietness of the end

I saw it first-hand
that crossing over to a promised land

It was his time to die
I held his hand and said goodbye
and with the arrival of death
I witnessed that last breath...

After retiring early, I now have the time to follow some interests -
I am Just starting out in trying poetry
Allpoetry.com/Mark.S.Man

[David I Mayerhoff]

The Bribe to Mediocre

the terror of inertia
lures the gullible
with the bait of an award

like acid rain eating at the pavement
the only forward thrust
is the rot in the belly of the poet

who longs to express
the fetid decay of the surrounding culture
in swollen tones of
death and warts

and does not slink
away from the real
into the feel-good tripe
of candy and Valium

he challenges the masses
to the Bullfight of progress
charging with smoke of rage
from the nostrils of status quo

if only the caricature
of Popeye
smoking his pipe of conquest

could be enough to satiate
the poetic gut

no rest from the
swelling within
that rumbling to burst forth
in song of antihero

instead growling the tune
of potential
unloved and unwept

soldiering on
to the chorus of the magnetic
who scheme to ply out the next Laureate
with laminated words
and stale echoes

David I Mayerhoff is an emerging literary writer, established scientific author, and a Clinical Professor of Psychiatry. He grew up on Long Island and now resides in New Jersey.
Allpoetry.com/David_Mayerhoff

[Raymond Huffman]

My Mountain

High on the ridge of the mountain
a thin line of red appears and shimmers in the dark
where it should be black
white smoke in the moonlight
alarms the sleeping birds
I have always lived here in the canyon
surrounded by pine trees
and the swift flowing stream far below
how many fires in the fireplace have there been
with the windows open to the cool mountain air
listening to owls
and the faint rustling of unknown creatures in the ground litter
who never worried me
or even of the report of a sighting of a cougar
I have left my window open at night near my pillow
and in the morning the snow has dusted my head
a cold man
loving the cold
and the wind
but now the wind brings the red line down
the red line becomes a palette of fire
advancing slowly at first
there is a sound like thunder
but it is not thunder
it is the sound of trees exploding

faster and faster the fire advances
now roaring through my canyon
there is no escape except down to the stream
but the stream is now steaming and hot from the fire
the stream boils
a deer races through the smoke screaming
the owls have long flown
the fire descends
I have been betrayed
by my mountain

_____

Raymond Huffman is a retired entomologist. He has been
writing and reading poetry for many years, but only now is just
beginning to dare to call himself a poet.
Allpoetry.com/Raymond_Huffman

[Lisa F. Raines]

Springtime study

Brooks bubble under
the springtime sun, and
bring a refreshing return
to beautiful blossoms,
budding branches, and
glorious green growth.

Bustling bees build
a burgeoning beehive,
as they bring back
powdery pollen
between blustery breezes.

Birds fly and sing
with artful abandon,
as they whirl and twirl,
frolic and flirt among
the forming folds
of fertile foliage.

They chase a siren song, and,
finding each other,
fanciful foreplay leads to
nuzzling in a new nest, and
the laying of expectant eggs.

AlisRamie is from North Carolina, USA.

Interests include: philosophy, history, international relations, poetry, art, design, jazz, funk rock, and some good old soul.

Allpoetry.com/AlisRamie

[Paul Hernandez]

Love's Memory

Walking hand and hand along the shoreline of the lake, taking in
the beauty of the mountain's rugged landscape.

Look how it's mirrored image softly reflects across the water so
elegantly.

We then stood single file, you in front of me facing the stillwater.

With both of my arms wrapped around your waist, we watched as
the sun started it's final descent from the evening sky.

While standing behind you, I could smell the
Lilac and Lavender fragrance in your hair,
mixed with the evening brisk air of Pine and Sage.

This will forever be etched in the memory of my love's reason for
missing you.

Mezmorized in silence by the bright vivid shades
of orange, gold and reds that glistened from the surface of the
water, all we could do was gaze.

Then, slowly, the sun sank into the lake until it was gone,
allowing the moon to softly light her now darkened sky.

Yes, I still long for moments like these with you.

The only true currency in this bankrupt world is what you share with someone else when you're uncool.
Lester Bangs

Being truthful and inspirational to yourself first is awe-inspiring to others.
Allpoetry.com/PaulyWally

[Alwyn Barddylbach]

Ethereal Thunder

Speak one to one and know not what I am -

How incidental was thy random birth,
beaten, bruised and banished, kingdom come!
Vented from the darkness reckless earth,
this universal rock the maker's surf.

Atom by atom, ion to ion incandescent
stellar sanctum, time my arbiter dwarfs
our solemn void of fractured space, argent
pillars of thunder in this mountain place.

Speak of ancients forever as I am shall be,
cloud of eons cluster, spiral fountains bliss,
Brahman deaf and blind as conscious matter.
Hush now, be still and quiet, dark almighty

[~I]listen![~IX]

Listen to that endless raging cosmic chatter

[~I]mercurial as we are.[~IX]

विचारों में शून्य के विस्तार से, अनंत को सैंयम से समेट लूंगा। - Fill the
void with mindfulness, cover the divine in peace: What gods and
ghosts you can imagine. Hush now, final incarnation, sonnet. -
AB Blue Mountains Allpoetry.com/Barddylbach

[Grace M Wells]

Gentle White Wisps

Chipped broken nails
on crimson fingertips
Chewed to the skin,
gnawed, blistered lips,
Unseeing eyes
laid in a sunken face,
Frail arms strewn
in delicate form,
Soft dandelion puffs
fly off to the blue abyss,
Notice their soar
lifted of their weight.

Grace is a young poet and author of several poetry collections. She enjoys rainy days, reading books, and warm bowls of ramen. Feel free to contact her gmwellsbooks@gmail.com.
Allpoetry.com/gmwells

[Ryan Grobler]

Unwritten

That lemon you left on the doorstep should have been sour
Not sweet from the bitterness you portrayed
A framed picture of a lady holding an umbrella
She looks for sunshine but finds only rain
Remembering fenced fields that were green on your side
Painted horses chasing clouds, filled with your imagination
Falling night skies bring change to unbalanced scales
Trailing wishes that illuminate paths shaping the next chapter.

Born and raised in Africa, now living in the USA. Self-made entrepreneur, currently CEO of national energy saving company. Writing poetry allows me to get away from the stresses of everyday life. Allpoetry.com/Grobbs

[Jim Beitman]

[Our kitty has lots of toys]

Our kitty has lots of toys
Feathery mice and glittery balloons
Flipping and tossing them up in the air
Chasing and hiding them under the chair
She has bells in balls
And a stuffed star and moon
But her favorite toy of all
Is just a plastic spoon

I am an artist living in Noblesville Indiana. Writing is a great media that helps distill my feelings, thoughts, and experiences. It is always a great thrill to be included in an Allpoetry anthology! Allpoetry.com/Beitmanjim

[Rebecca Friend]

Who are you, and what have you done with

my body?

Don't you just hate the fracas
when body parts betray us,
organs grow traitorous,
vessels of clay and dust?

Like when my tongue,
pumped up on tonic and rum,
talks out of turn,
that muscle-headed bum
jumps in line
ahead of my mind
and stutters those

three little words,

or when my fingers get burned
after they squirm
to do the walking,
no amount of talking
can stop them from stroking
those flames of red hair from
his hazel-grey eyes.

Hot-wired neurons
misfire
when a kiss from him
burrows under my skin,
a novel parasite
that births butterflies overnight
spreading ecstasy
neck to knee,
leaving me down alice's rabbit hole,

or up eve's tree,

too happy to bite the apple
labeled [~I]*eat me*[~IX]...
a battle sweet
as limbs slip and slide,
warm fronts collide,
heartbeats overheat and
shout out [~I]*hoorah*[~IX],
when love stages a coup d'état
on the brain.

Don't you just hate that?

––––––––––––––

Mother, grandmother, social worker and liberal hippie from
North Carolina...
I found my voice in poetry. Allpoetry.com/Becki_Friend

[Lorri Ventura]

A Child's Dreams

In her dreams she drives an ice cream truck
And hands free fudgsicles to all the children
She cures cancer
Ends wars
Reverses climate change
And speaks all languages fluently.
She spreads kernels of beauty and hope
Wherever she goes
The way Miss Rumphius blanketed the earth
With lupine seeds
Best of all
She lives in a house full of cats
That purr her to sleep at night
So that she can save the world

-

_____

Lorri Ventura is a retired special education administrator living in Massachusetts. Her writing has been featured in a number of anthologies. Allpoetry.com/Lorri_Ventura

[Dorianna Ric]

Black Slime Oozes

there's a deadly black slime
oozing its sprawly tentacles
in and around my blood cells
twisting into corners
burrowing into every crevice
carrying debilitating disease
dumping excruciating pain
till my spirit wants to die

I close my eyes to sleep
a grotesque slimy black oozing
twisting its way behind my eyes
making a trail through brain cells
crushing the will to live
I hear its deadly whisper
in my dream like slumber
commanding me to die
I struggle to rise up
to fight another day

Dorianna is a story teller, song writer and nature lover. In nature she finds inspiration and words become poems. She writes about life as experienced, dissected and observed.
Allpoetry.com/DoriannaRic

[Boasa Ft Otineru]

Bend in the wind

There is a honey bee I see
hung by the taste and smell of
nectar
in the flowers
around a little branch that
bends in the wind

the flowers sway in the tip
purple and pretty
sweet no doubt
that is why the bee hangs
around them
for too long

both the bee and I
face a large wall painting
tracing the multi racial world
well very befittingly given that we both are
in a visitor information center
in an exotic variety garden

the painting is quite beautiful
highlighting the world
a bold leaning tower somewhere
in Europe

a pretty ballad dancer in a perfect
toe stance and butterfly dress

a strong Scottish looking woman
messy hair black dress
doing a crazy leg dance
there is a mosque in Moscow and
a Mexican masquerading
a bull below the Eiffel Tower
a London bridge that will not burn ever

above all this is a controversy
a canoe that flies a starlight flag
but lined with war shields of the Vikings
were vikings much more than we know?
this I have not paid mind to before in
quite a tropical garden of this beauty

I readily felt a smell of
lavish soothe and green munificence
thickets of lavender
dark brow tea leaf and reddish pink roses and
two tall tamarinds looming
like giants at the gates

yet my soul is drawn back
to the pretty purple flowers
sweet and juicy with nectar
green eucalyptic leaves
and the bee still hangs by

that little branch tip
bend in the wind.

I am a Samton, Samoa Tongan who loves writing and
photography as both passion and art. Life is a journey of joy and is
meant to be written for all to enjoy. I love you, who is reading
this? Allpoetry.com/Boasa_FT_Otineru

[Catherine Jean Lindsey Towery Sales]

Four Hundred Years

Four Hundred Years

Of Blood Sweat
and Tears
And you
trying to give
Twenty eight days
To celebrate being
A Black slave
Only in Amerikkka

Four hundred Years

Begging, Borrowing
And stealing
Beaten down
Hung up
Strung up
Shackles on
My feet
Crumbs on
my table
For over

Four hundred years

Of Tasting my tears
Running Down
my face
While i Cry out
Jesus Jesus Jesus
My only hope
For salvation
And still you
refuse
To give us
Our Reprivation

Four Hundred years

We toiled and labored
In your fields
Being fed
the Crumbs
From your
table
While you raped
Our women
And killed
Our men
With mass
incarceration
Giving us
Dope to cope
Little to no hope
Still You refuse

to acknowledge
This Atrocity
refusing to
Grant us
Reprivation
You only give
A weak ass
apology
That does
not satisfy me
Or anyone
For theSe
Atrocities

Four hundred years

Of Slavery
Misery
Abuse
Misuse
Oppression
Depression
Compression
Discrimination
Injustice
Inequality
We're not askinb
We demand
our Reprivation
For all Four

Hundred years
Filled with abuse
And tears

Four hundred years

Of Slavery
Poverty
Misery
Slavery
Nightmares
Still hunt me
Mass incarceration
Discrimination
Double standard
Jim Crow laws
full of Injustice
Lack of education
Deprivation
Reprivation
Would be Just
the beginning
Of an effort to
Apologize
To our people
For

Four Hundred Years

Of Slavery
Toiling day
And night
In your
Cotton fields
How bout that
Reprivation?
Help us to
forgive
So we can
heal
From this
Pain and misery?

Catherine Sales former Ed Counselor from Compton
CA.Catherine holds several Master's Degree in
Psychology,Education,Human Behavior,& Education Adm Cred.
Former President PA4C M.H .Advocacy 501C.
Allpoetry.com/Cathysalesmftpoet

[Miss Rachel Anne]

mydreamday

i dream of the day,

wearing my hip-flares,

and my bunny-Galaxy top,

with my bunny walking down the path beside me,

feeling the nature sand & hearing the blue ocean nearby,

this is my ideal dreamday full of ocean seashell sounds, and the

waves,

as i walk down with a few looking faces,

listening to quiet dancing pop music,

as i walk down the path with a single blue flower,

where i meet the man in his casual clothes,

with a smile on his face,

as we both dance a little,

because today is the day,

for that

forever blue bloom

_____

MissRachelanne is from Western Australia. Poetry is a passion and & love writing as a way of expressing thoughts & ideas. Allpoetry.com/ForeverBloompoetry

[Stephen Hollins]

the tsunami's bones

black hooves spin in slow-mo

in white howling mountain brrr

spring's gold voice melts snow

I live on beautiful Waiheke Island in New Zealand. I specialize in Improv for theatre, dance, clown, mime, teaching adults to become more playful, building and renovation. Allpoetry.com/Stephen_Hollins

Misty, The Surprise Kitten

Licorice, our solid black cat,
survived a skunk attack
vivid yellow eyes squinting
a bath with tomato sauce ensued

This cat got stuck in storm drain in the dark of night
neighbors out at 3 a.m.,
a warbling wail of the trapped feline
three men lifting the grate to the sewer
out he bounds out, chasing freedom
like a tickling hair on his butt

moving from Pennsylvania to Texas
he handled the kennel ride just fine
at the hotel, he was meowing on the bed
Licorice reared up towards my father's face
a spray of urine covered my parents
yelling and chaos went on for about an hour

there came a time when Licorice
got very sick, moaning as only an sick cat can
before the end of the day, he had died.

we begged my parents for a new cat
but it was one rainy day my father

who had on his silver work raincoat,
walked home from the carpool stop

father called for my brother and I
he kept the buttons closed
then there was movement
hearing a little meow

my father opened his jacket
a rough grey and black tabby kitten peeked out
we were so surprised and ecstatic
grabbing my father in a hug
we pet the tiny, wet kitten
Misty became her name

Marta Green is from the state of TX. Her passions are writing
poetry and short stories. She lives with her husband, son and
several fur babies. Allpoetry.com/Marta_Green

[Chukwuebuka Emmanuel Obi]

Dream beyond dreams

Dream among dreams
sound clashing like symbols
raindrops fall into an ocean
like sand dust dropping on a desert

I was thrown from the ship
like Jonah without fish
sinking fast like pins
ships appearing so small
like a pair of shoes

this dream is beyond grim
cries everywhere
like a teardrop falls
into an ocean

between mermaid's fists
led to the cage of serpent
bitten by one upon another
till I danced the music
dance of the dead

dreams upon dreams
everything seem like magic
like candle wax falling
into hot oil

I try to wake up
all the more I dream
with less control over
what it unfolds

dream above dreams
wrestling with the unknown
echoes of time
falling off my eyes

Chukwuebuka is a Nigerian. He is a member of martial arts and loves aquarium. An Entrepreneur who enjoys writing stories, ideas and poems. Allpoetry.com/Obiekwe_Emmanuel

[David I Mayerhoff]

Looking Up, Looking Down

Tonight as I gaze upon the stars
a scintilla of nostalgia crosses the eye
at the planet Jupiter

into the heavens soaring
the burden of memory
ignites the flame of passion for the sky's drama

in what hopes to be
the next frame of the skylight
stars explode in raw power

burdening friend and foe
with the caution
of what is looking down upon them

is that frown I see in the stars' pattern,
posing as spectator
reproving the false prophets

a bubble surrounds the sheltered
not wishing to tumble
into the plains of battle

a devil may care
if one can find the enemy
out here beyond the grasp

David I Mayerhoff is an emerging literary writer, established scientific author, and a Clinical Professor of Psychiatry. He grew up on Long Island and now resides in New Jersey.
Allpoetry.com/David_Mayerhoff

[Michael Bud Frensley]

Death Measurement

your measurement will dictate how much time you have,

your height and weight divided by three,
will tell you your death measurement,
your measurement is divided by three for the three final death
acts.

you must be fully grown around age twenty-four to be correctly
measured.
all heights and weights are measured in this way for death
measurement.
Your death measurement will fluctuate with your height and
weight.
death measurement works for both males and females.

If you are 4' foot 0" inches tall, and you weighed 124 lbs pounds,
you would add 4 to 0 making 40, then you would add 40 to 124
equaling 164 divided by 3, equaling 54.66666666666667,
and that would be the age of your death,
and nothing could interrupt this.

If you four foot eleven inches tall, 4' 11", and weighed 134 lbs
pounds, you would add 0022 to the eleven before adding the
height to the weight, when adding eleven inches to any height
footage there must be a decimal point between the foot and the
inches, 4.110022 plus 134, equals, 138.110022 divided by 3, equals,

46.036674, and that would be the age of your death, and nothing could interrupt this.

If you are 4' 10", four foot ten inches tall, you would add 02 to the 10 inches and a decimal point in between the 4 foot and the 10 inches,
4.1002, and you weighed 143 lbs, you would add 143 to 4.1002 equaling 147.1002 divided by 3 equals 49.0334, and that is the age of your death and nothing can interrupt this.

if you are 4' 6" four foot six inches tall and weighed 96 lbs pounds, you would add 46 plus 96 equaling 142, divide 142 by 3 equaling 47.333333, and that would be the age of your death, and nothing could interrupt this..

if you are five foot even 5' you would add a zero at the end of five 5 to make five zero 50,
it will look like the number fifty 50,
if you weighed one hundred and thirty pounds 130lbs,
you would add one hundred and thirty pounds 130 lbs to five zero 50,
making a total calculation equaling one hundred and eighty 180,
divide one hundred and eighty 180 by three, equaling sixty 60,
and that would be the age of that persons death,
and nothing could interrupt this.

if you are five foot nine inches 5'9" tall,
you would calculate five nine 59,
plus weight of said person which is two hundred and eighty nine pounds 289lbs,
five nine 59 plus two eighty nine equals three hundred and forty

eight 348,

divide three hundred and forty eight 348 by three, equaling one hundred and sixteen 116,

and that is the age of my death and nothing can interrupt this.

.10" inches looks like this .1002,

02, zero two is added to the number 1 that's in this equation

.11" inches looks like this .110022,

0022, zero zero two two is added for the number 1's in this equation.

if you are five ten 5'10" five foot ten inches tall,

you would calculate five point one zero zero two,

5.1002 and your weight two hundred and ten pounds 210lbs to five point one zero zero two 5.1002

equaling two hundred and fifteen point one zero zero two 215.1002 divided by three equals

71.70006666666667 and that is your age of death and nothing can interrupt this.

if you are five foot eleven inches tall 5'11",

you would calculate five point one one zero zero two two,

5.110022 and you weighed three hundred pounds 300lbs you would calculate five point one one zero zero two two and you would add that measurement to three hundred 300,

equaling three hundred and five point one one zero zero two two 305.110022, then,

you would divide that by three,

equaling one hundred and one point seven zero three three four zero six six six six six six seven 101.7033406666667,

and that is the age of your death and no one can interrupt this..

1 oz is calculated as 102,
1 inch is calculated as 102

if a human is 9" inches tall the calculation would be 902,
and the human weighed 4 ounce's the calculation would be 402,
902 + 402 = 1304 divided by 3 = 434.6666667 years before that
human dies.

If you are 5' foot exactly you would put 50 as your calculation and
for 6' foot even 60.

so if you are 5 foot 0 inches the calculation would look like this 50,
if you weighed 150 pounds the calculation would be 150,
50 + 150 = 200 divided by 3 equals 66.66666666666667,
and that age will be the age of your death and nothing can
interrupt this

If someone says they're 74,
and they weigh 130lbs
and they are 5' foot 1" tall,
and I do the math,
of death measurement, 51 plus 130 = 181 divided by 3 = 60.3333333,
this person should have passed away already or do they carry a
false birth certificate making them appear older?

if you are 5' foot 10" the calculation would be 5.1002 and if you
weighed 230lbs,
5.1002 plus 230 equals 235.1002 divided by 3 equals 78.3667333, and
that is your age of death and nothing can interrupt this.

if you are 5' foot 11" the calculation would be 5.110022,
and you weighed 300lbs,

5.110022 plus 300 equals 305.110022 divided by 3 equals 101.703341,
and that is your age of death and nothing can interrupt this.

if you are 17' foot even you will calculate 170 as your height plus
your weight which we are going to say is 300 pounds so 170 plus
300 = 470 divided by 3 = 156.666667,
and that is your age of death 156 and nothing can interrupt this..

if you are 16' foot 4" you will calculate 164 as your height,
and say you weighed 284 so, 164 plus 284 = 448 divided by 3 =
149.333333,
and that is the age of your death and nothing can interrupt this..

if you are 16' foot 10" you will calculate 16.1002 and you weighed
220lbs you will add 16.1002 to 220 = 236.1002 divided by 3 =
78.7000667,
and that is your age of death and nothing can interrupt this..

if you are 15' foot 11" your calculation will be 15.110022 and if you
weighed 234lbs,
15.110022 plus 234 = 249.110022 divided by 3 = 83.036674,
and that is the age of your death and nothing can interrupt this.
Death measurement..

––––––––––––––––––

Bird, Brings, Death, Fly, Brings, Life...
Allpoetry.com/death_show

[Doctor Laura C. Locet]

Bodies dance

Bodies dance, Spirits gone, Past dancing when all else has gone.

Life's limp body stiffens like wood. Piled high are the dead, Life's skins have been shed.

Our dead we no longer bury we haven't lost the time.

Our trucks dance past the windows of streets eyes passing the time, Life is over but only for the dead.

See your friends from 6feet only it is said.

Mom, Poet, Artist, Doctor of Theology, New Yorker who used to do performance for a living... Former model as well as straight forward kind, Fire, patient enough, honest and kind until time is up 1986. Allpoetry.com/Loc-et-nyc

[Uma Asopa]

Mango dreams

A part of me is a bird
nestled in the wind's rustle
attempting to lift and rise
to reach the highest perch
on a mango's canopy
to unravel
what once used to be ---
myself, a weak winged daydream
swinging on a bed
of pollen powered panicles
budding little mangoes
transiting to their fleshy self
in a season when nothing else
mattered, but a lovelorn
fragrance of home, lost
in climatic turns

where I once lived with my peers,
the kindred spirits ---
some other birds
could be boisterous parrots
or impatient sunbirds

they are very much there,
as I am looking for myself ---
I have lost track of my nest.

I am a retired pediatrician. I live in Gujarat, a western state of India with my family.

Poetry has been an integral part of my routine for a long ti AP an inspiring platform to write and read poetry.

Allpoetry.com/Uma71

[Deborah F Thomas]

Betrayed

Snowflake promises
ensconced in rain
mortal drips inflicting pain
of constant dribble of wet remorse
as his heart slowly strays from course

A skillfully painted masterpiece
that turned a hunger into a feast
A glass of wine - a toast to us
Tin man's tears now glean with rust

Unfaithful to the wedding vows
Discarded monogrammed white towels
A crumpled license signed by two
No hand in mine when death blows through

I've never felt so more betrayed
then being part of his charade

Deborah is a senior citizen who writes rhyming poetry in her
spare time from a small town in Maryland. Loves the written
word, cats and her three daughters.
Allpoetry.com/Deborah_F_Thomas

[Tisham Dhar]

Unter Boss

Lights radiate into space
From earth, home base.
Gum trees twist up to star
White barks reaching up far,
Like a very slow star boat
In the oceans of time they float.

Passengers on spaceship earth
Humans tend to home and hearth.
Suomi and ISS watch the city lights,
Merging with bushfires some nights.
House and entire towns a complete loss,
We battle nature, the final boss.

Nations battle each other,
Innocents, the shells smother.
Why has it come to this?
The unter-boss, human hubris!

Tisham is an Electrical and Electronics Engineer, twice failed Dr.
(MBBS/PhD).
He likes signal processing and generates all sorts of patterns
including rhymes and poetry. Allpoetry.com/Tisham_Dhar

[William La Civita]

Car Trouble

A rattle below the horizon
A click, a grind, I stop
With the sacrificial smoke
In an empty parking lot.
How I wish to ride away
And comprehend the mist,
And smash the clattering steel,
Battle dust that chokes the world,
And taste the coming flood.
I sit for minutes, broken.

Retired, gay, married, working-class: I have been writing poetry for years, but I never showed it to anyone. This is my new venture out of the poetry closet. Allpoetry.com/Blll

[Jim Beitman]

[The kitties woke up early]

The kitties woke up early
Playing carnival games last night
Unconcerned about the time
They began their morning flight
By scampering around
Bopping and hopping
Batting and dodging
Right side up
And upside down
The volume increased
As they became ready to feast
Meowing loudly
In the breakfast room
Hissing and swishing
To get a good spot
Prancing and dancing
And smiling a lot
Munching and crunching
And licking their feet
Now they're content
To go back to sleep

I am an artist living in Noblesville Indiana. Writing is a great media that helps distill my feelings, thoughts, and experiences. It is always a great thrill to be included in an Allpoetry anthology! Allpoetry.com/Beitmanjim

[Lisa F. Raines]

They fight for us!

Mothers, wives, children of Ukraine
We see you say, "Where are we?" "Where will we go?"
"We don't know anyone in Poland, or Slovakia, or Romania!"

You look up from the cold station floor
Watching as desperate people shuffle by
Following the dirty cement escape route

They don't see each other, or you, or me
The silent, cold, alone, and confused refugees
Are still one people united, Ukrainian

Husbands, sons, fathers
Sunflowers in the field
Scared, but standing strong

Willing to die for their families
To die for their neighbors
To die for their homes, lands, and country

Armed with Molotov Cocktails
A most basic weapon
Civilians face the Russian tanks

United, they fight the Russian tyrant
They fight for their democracy
For the rights of all democracies

They fight for all of us!

AlisRamie is from North Carolina, USA.
Interests include: philosophy, history, international relations,
poetry, art, design, jazz, funk rock, and some good old soul.
Allpoetry.com/AlisRamie

[Marjorie Buyco]

Broken Vases

Mother was always chasing
what can never be found
she sits on her dilapidated throne
that looks beaten like her skin

bruises of different stages of
healing shaped a topography
where his hands left imprints
of his troubled past

his words can tear down
a mountain, it is in this cave
where she hides
curled to her feet

and as always in the aftermath
he would cover the ground
she walks on with pretty Daffodils
kiss her lips a taste of Cherry Wine

but it is every day that I find
broken vases on her doorstep
I keep the pieces in my pocket
hoping one day I can patch
these among the surge of morning waves:

She will become
whole again

_____

Marjorie Buyco is from the Philippines but is now residing in
Illinois. Journal and poetry writing gives her a venue for self-
reflection and self-expression. Allpoetry.com/Goldistring

[Derek Hubbard]

Growing through Changes

On a distant horizon lie my last living days
Where I go from there hopefully will amaze
My body's gone so I'll be one with my mind
I would like to leave a little bit of me behind

Bury me in tater sacks in dirt rich with loam
Out back on the ten acres behind my home
Cover me over then plant a lil sapling tree
For another hundred years I'll be feeling free

I'll spread pollen in spring, leaves in the fall
Grow a full canopy more than fifty feet tall
I'll sow some seed, have kids far and wide
Forest of my family across the countryside

When I'm old and tired and about to break
Chop me down and build a cabin by a lake
Face me towards a cove would be my wish
So I can see the water with the jumping fish

When it's weathered and it's about to cave
Take it down and bury it in a lakeside grave
Say words of wisdom then just walk away
I'll listen for big fish to plop on a sunny day

I've been writing poetry, mostly rhymes, for almost fifty years. I like exploring the human condition and trying to relay that in a way that people can relate to. Allpoetry.com/Charlie'sWaiting

[Paul Crocker]

Trees Of Fire

Today I saw many trees of different sizes.
I looked up in wonder at how tall each one rises.
The colours that adorned every little twig.
If inspiration was food then call me a pig.

As if each branch was covered in flame.
And with what splendor and triumph it came.
So bright and warm as though from a lit match.
The similarities to the eye, what a catch.

The breeze moving the leaves like flickering embers.
A moment that every eyewitness remembers.
The fallen leaves of course were lava under our feet.
But we had no cares as we kicked up the molten heat.

———————————

I am a poet from Bristol, UK. I started writing poems in 2001. I enjoy both reading and writing poetry and everything connected with it. Allpoetry.com/PoeticXscape

[Kathryn Wiepking]

Altars In the Woods

sunlight falls upon

moss adorning aging stumps

altars in the woods

Kathryn Wiepking is from Wisconsin. I love being outside and experiencing the world through all the little details one can find when looking closely. Allpoetry.com/Kate_W

[Vicki Moore]

Rain Shower Memories

I always sit outside in the rain,
remembering you, my love;
taking our showers in the rain,
water flowing over your skin,
dripping like diamonds
from the ends of your dark hair.
Circling your seashell ear,
my tongue made you shiver;
your breath like a hurricane wind
as I gently kiss the petals
that were your pink lips.
I still remember the feel of you,
soft as our satin sheets;
slick with water.
The scent of jasmine and freesia
we used as our bed.
Making love in the flowers
could not compare to the sweet scent
of your neck or your inner thighs.
I still miss your tinkling laugh,
like Christmas bells,
and the way you whispered my name,
soft as flying angel wings.
I always sit outside in the rain,
remembering you, my love;

the rain showers join my tears
as I weep by your grave.

_____

I am a 60 year old woman learning to express myself with poetry.
I started writing in High School but stopped for many years. I
have survived many things but I have never given up hope.
Allpoetry.com/Vicki_moore

[Marta E Green]

Shhhhhhhh, The Forest Is Alive

crystal coated pine

white snow iridescent shine

effervescent light

Marta Green lives in the state of Texas. Her passions are writing poetry and short stories. She lives with her husband and son as well as several fur babies. Allpoetry.com/Marta_Green

[Nancy Lee Armstrong]

A Christmas Surprise

At Christmas time I have a surprise for my son
he had these medal Tonka Trucks as a child,
he played with them near the road in a dirt pile
me and my husband decided to refurbish them
after trucks rusted lying out in the pouring rain
he sanded off all the paint and wiped the dust,
then primed them where you no longer had rust
my husband had no experience to paint them
I took the parts to tucks collision and restoration
to a professional painter who knew their stuff
the big surprise was he didn't charge me much
when I received them back they looked like new,
it was such a magical moment and exciting too
I think Christmas is a time for everyone to enjoy
they are fun and exciting for every girl and boy
this gift of his will be, put under the Christmas tree
be given as a token of my love forever a memory.

––––––––––––––

This poem is about my son, Jeff who played with them
at the age of four. I had them refurbished forty-one
years later and gave them to him for a Christmas gift.
This was a nice surprise. Allpoetry.com/Nanarm45

[Chad Hebner]

I Remember

I try to think of places
Of my childhood gone by
Running through the fields
Or finding places to hide

Now my days grow shorter
Those places mean more and more
Sitting watching the sunset
On the dock above the shore

There was an old pear tree
In my grandmothers' yard when I was small
I would climb it to see the world
And I thought I could see it all

The lake so blue with its waves
The mountains rising behind
Are now just a mere painting
In my loud and failing mind

I remember walking the train tracks
Anywhere I wanted to go
With my bicycle tire bouncing on the wood
Or crunching in the snow

I remember sitting on the pier
Down at Lucy park
With the remnant of a past carnival
That left their indelible mark

I remember sitting on a bench
And watching the world go by
Never knowing that one day
It would be my time to say goodbye

Chad Hebner is originally from Jamestown, NY. He is the father
of three daughters, who are his world. Poetry and painting are his
creative outlet. Allpoetry.com/Chad_Hebner

[Carla Horne]

Beautiful Fear

Shades of black beauty
touch colorful dimensions
of tomorrow
blind to fear.

Beautiful black,
the absence of light,
dances with all colors,
adorns all people,
until
Fear is born
from the union of
the unseen and the unknown.

Take your fear,
take it down,
recognize it for what it is.

And when stars are pinned
to the darkest night,
dance in black organdy
around the ballroom
entranced by black's duality:
beauty and fear.

I am a Southerner from Georgia, and have lived most of my life near coastal Savannah. As a poet, I see poetry as a form of art that helps preserve our history. Thank you for reading our poetry. Allpoetry.com/Crafty_Mermaid

Old Missy

With an owl as her guard dog,
Staying up all night,
He turns his head round and round,
Making sure everything is alright,
A steed as her taxi,
Driving her all over town,
She makes sure to stop so he can drink,
Just so she can still get around,
Dressed in a cabaret fashion she travels,
Impressing on some, yet detestable to others,
Flowers are flair for her ruffled-up skirt,
Hosiery and a top hat complete her druthers,
With no need for a purse,
The city feeds her money,
No heed for any curse,
She does not find that funny,
She is the boss lady, the chief, and the captain,
Nothing goes without her say or else it does not happen,
In an industrial venture, she brings money in,
The 19th century is where it all begins,
Her picture still stands in the 21st century now,
She is still a valued figurehead someway or somehow,
Steampunk you might say would be the word of the day,
Still, this little old miss likes to come out and play.

Glenn Folkes got his graduate degree from the University of North Texas. He still writes poetry and music.
Allpoetry.com/Barkdream69

[Jeanette Showalter]

Silent Black, Talking Back

Black is spooky in a cave.
Hushed and solemn at a grave.
An outcast from society -
the lone black sheep variety.

In a dress, it slims the hips.
Goth when worn on nails and lips.
The shroud that lays the dead away.
Come hither sexy lingerie.

The airplane box whose secrets tell
what went wrong and why it fell.
Mail that threatens and demands.
Blacking out right where we stand.

For a necktie, formal wear.
The bad guy hat; heroes beware!
A belt worn by a martial artist.
The color of the evil hearted.

Our morning coffee love affair.
A hole in space to who knows where.
Secrets, magic, vigilance,
evil, death, and elegance.

In a subtle silent way,
from raven black to charcoal grey;
black sure had a lot to say!

———————————

Hailing from New York, Jaye Showalter writes from San Diego, CA. She began writing stories and doodling to entertain her children and their friends. Allpoetry.com/Jaye_Showalter

[S. Libellule]

A Touch of Grey

There is so much to say
about this touch of grey
barefooted steps
wading through ashes of regret
unable to forget
all the bridges burnt
leaving me here
shedding a tear

on this side of the poem

Libellule is originally from New England and now lives outside Birmingham, Alabama. The poet writes about nature, authenticity, and the examined life. Influences include Mary Oliver and Billy Collins. Allpoetry.com/Little_Dragonfly

[RJ Kram]

the light of night

tiny firefly

beneath the full white moon,

a shooting star

My name is Mark. I write and paint under the name RJ Kram. It's a name I've carried with me for a long time that originated from a little joke. I have a beautiful wife and two bright little girls. Allpoetry.com/RJ_Kram

[Kei Ku]

someday i will love myself

seeds of failure sown
ingrained to be rejected
shame
to be buried in its unmarked grave

but engrave– its beginning
struggling stumbling
forward
to self excavating

love i had buried away
once volatile
will ossify one day–
settling to stay

Keiku is an oncology pharmacist and avid hobbyist who writes in
their free time– each poem is its own little universe with its own
truths– writing or reading a poem is a new and fresh beginning.
Allpoetry.com/keiku

[David Flynn]

the rays of the sun were tangible in her eyes

as if some journey bespoke in a dream
and the moon white and prismatic overhead
directed every step of her path twirling it
around the stars
her aim to stay young and thwart the years
bleeding them of all their wisdom
as if the deeds of every mortal turned to dust

Hello, I have written 284 poems between 2019 and 2021. My career is in medicine but I have a strong interest in the arts. flynnpoetry.com Please enjoy ! David. Allpoetry.com/David_Flynn

[Peter Zdrenka]

Sahara

The blazing sun scorches the dry golden sand.
Up above, a Red-Tailed Hawk screeches it echo's for miles
yet not another sound..
The intense heat waves add to the stillness
giving it a more desolate eerie and lonely place to be.
Yet it is so beautiful to see.
It is where the sun shines it's heart out
and the rain cowers on the outskirts afraid to enter it's domain.
I stand on the edge of the Sahara and gaze into its openness
to afraid to enter.

Born 1963 in Liverpool England, in 1982 I travelled to South
Afrika. I now live back in the uk in Preston, Lancashire, Uk. I
write poetry for the release of emotions. Allpoetry.com/Zedy

[Peter Zdrenka]

Our Innocent Years

My childhood years and times gone by,
I remember them well when I was a child,
Eating ice cream and playing hide and seek,
climbing trees and scuffed knees,
Apple pie my gran baked,
Toffee apples and strawberry cake,
The magic we shared with imaginative glee,
Father Christmas
and the Tooth Fairy,
For them only to fade as we age,
our imaginative
thoughts are taken away,
They teach us in school of how we should be,
To grow up and take responsibility. But as I get older I'd much
sooner be,
back as a child with my imaginative side,
I'd imagine a life different to this no more worries a life of bliss.

––––––––––––––––––

born in Liverpool England 1963 travelled to South Afrika in 1982
now living back in the uk in Preston Lancashire uk write poetry
for release of emotions Allpoetry.com/Zedy

.

[Carla Horne]

Never Thought

I woke up this morning,
wondering where I
was going
so far from home.

Two dollars in my pocket
looking for a highway to the sea
tripped over an old bucket
and skinned my knee.

Picked up a few dollars
helping a guy unload hay.
Pulled up my collar
headed to the Chesapeake Bay.

Been gone for so long
Never thought like this
that it could all go so wrong.
Never knew it was our last kiss.

———————————

Hi, I am the Crafty Mermaid, and I started writing poetry in
middle school. I then enjoyed teaching
English for twenty years. Now, I sincerely hope that you never
stop reading. Allpoetry.com/Crafty_Mermaid

[Lorri Ventura]

The End

The last man standing

After the apocalypse

Regrets surviving

Lorri Ventura is a retired special education administrator living in Massachusetts. Her writing has been featured in several anthologies. Allpoetry.com/Lorri_Ventura

[Thomas Hofmann]

Freedom Ride

I wake up in the morning,
Sun rising in the east,
Put on my leather jacket,
And climb aboard my beast,
Then I head on down the highway,
With no one else around,
Nobody can touch me now,
Because I'm freedom bound.

No more regulations,
No more lousy rules,
No one there to hold me back,
I'm nobody's fool,
Call me wild and radical,
Call me an outlaw,
It does not even bother me,
I've heard the freedom call.

I don't need no silver dollars,
I don't need no diamond rings,
For the world is wide with lots to see,
And I hear it beckoning,
Freedom is my mistress,
And she's always by my side,
Nobody can touch me now,
I'm on my freedom ride

Thomas is a lifelong resident of Michigan, currently living on a small lake in the southern part. His poetry is about many different subjects. When something inspires him, he writes a poem Allpoetry.com/Cowrider59

[Crystal McCollom]

222 Days of Light

143 days of darkness

twin flames of passionate presence dance
in perfect counterpoint
opening the fabric of the universe
a love letter scratched in parchment
of inky blackness
swallowing up the unknown

I grow wings and soar
searching
in insidious darkness
dream inspired
into an everlasting night
of floating sound

entrancing

slowing
falling towards the stars
soothing

suspending

when my sun goes to sleep
sweetened with ideal demise

after a long satisfying life
in celebration of you...

my heroes
I will forever be with you

when my sun goes to sleep
I lay me down for final rest

when my sun goes to sleep
I welcome an old friend

when my sun goes to sleep
[~I]a moment for the poet's play[~IX]
sorrow departs

I write poetry or need to write poetry when I am emotionally
aroused or sweating droplets of curiosity. 222 is a spiritual
number which is said to usher in new possibilities.
Allpoetry.com/Nannanorse

[David Hoare Holmes]

The Crucible Of Fire

We call it ash,
although it is more like
desiccated granular bone coral.
Whether ash or coral, I will be.

I am afraid, as I see through unseeing eyes,
as I feel, even though I cannot feel,
the flickering flames through the doors ahead,
waiting for what was me.

Young once,
not special, but a beginning, a promise.
No hill was too tall to climb, no challenge too great
no laughter too big to embrace.

Dreams.
And then desire shredded,
sent aloft with the winds
vanished to some other world.

My hands have grown spotted with time.
Eyes gone dim and rheumy,
sour old man breath of despair, and yes
magic, either forgotten or
tossed toward the fire ahead.

David Hoare Holmes is a retired health care worker who has published widely in various medical journals, has a long-term love of words and continues to explore word pictures in his poetry.
Allpoetry.com/David_Hoare_Holmes

[Mike Odavis]

Distant Reminder

An anxious feather,
began to hover,
over a frozen lake of glass.
Flying through fire,
ever so higher.
Into the memories of the long-forgotten past.
Soaring above the mountain tops
while slowly increasing speed.
The feather flew higher,
with a distant reminder.
Just how much a feather can see.
A gust of wind will take you anywhere.
If only the feather could receive.
A dash of hope,
a touch of atmosphere.
Some wind and the will to go where ever you please.

––––––––––––––

Mike Odavis is from Seattle Washington. Poetry is his way of coping with life's ups and downs. Mike likes to spend time at the ocean with his family. Allpoetry.com/Candyass

[Angela Burnham Spragg]

I Dance With Life

I danced today and flowed like a wave.
I felt my heart dancing with its feet.
My hips swayed like the sea waves, gently brushing against the
breeze of life.
I flowed and flowed,
swayed with each breath I inhaled and then exhaled.

My hand danced like wings thrusting the fluffy clouds,
Danced like the eagle swaying in the sky.
The dance of the month of July,
In the heat, it's a gentle breeze through my moist hair.
In the gentle breeze I swayed like the falling maple leaf.

The breeze beneath my feet carried me forward,
Carrying me like an angel floating and flying in the sky.
How gracious it is to dance with the breath,
The breath inside me and around, saturating every living cell.
So, I live to dance the tireless dance again.

———————————

Ms. Angela B. Spragg is from England, UK. She is an accredited
International Self-Perspective Coach. Her poems are about the
conversation with THE SELF. In the noise we forget THE SELF
has a voice. Allpoetry.com/Ms._Angela_B._Spragg

[Barbara Copley]

I have no words

I see you watching the neighbor
as she carries her baby into the house.
Longing. Family.
I am not enough
My womb, vacant,
condemned years ago as uninhabitable:
We are not enough
It's only in this moment that I contemplate regret
Pointless,
These thoughts of motherhood
These feelings of loss
for a never-to-be child

I sip coffee and deliberate what to say to you,
willing the steam to conjure a vision.
Like an incantation, I intone the uns:
Untangle my tongue,
Uncloud my sky,
Unclutter my closet,
Unsour my milk,
Unsee the sight
Three times, I repeat it
Three times, I censor the ache
with fidelity, both hands clasping the mug
My musing lingers too long;
the coffee's turned cold.
I have no words

Barbara lives with her husband and a brood of fur babies who
have adopted her as one of their own.
Allpoetry.com/Bobbie_D

[Terence O'Leary]

3121 CE - The Wrapes of Grath

The wrapes of Grath adorn the path that slammer klangks once tread
while turning spades in everglades to flosticate the dead.
Along the way the snorbels bay at freebled sprutelned
that boogeymen had once again uphove above the shed.

The buildings tall that housed the krawl are pictured carved in stone
since all that's left is now bereft of wrapes that might atone
for scabs that feed our wrinkled breed, distraught and lying prone.
Yes, flonk replaces merpeled traces deep inside, alone.

There's no retreat from incomplete, so durbies never dared,
but streaped instead beneath their bed with franjent fangs unbeared;
they knew the past could never last although the trumpets blared,
for doogies, stripped, were ill equipped, no longer bald or haired.

Like cavaliers with gougejent spears, well triggered for a tiff,
slank vankulures with silver spurs entglissed for grimp and griff
(no question why, for "we can't die", the oft regleated riff);
with little fuss the blunder bus krunged glimpfly off the cliff
and fetid breet of grim defeat gave Grath its final whiff;
the catapult had one result, all life lay lazelled stiff.

The plastic waves that washed the graves, now homeland for the
rutch,
though faring worse when quenching thirst with warples in the
hutch
were nonetheless, as frunks confess, so pleasant to the touch
exturbing sinks that watered wynx and onetime life as such.

Like burning blotters slurping waters, skindles sipped their fill
from koozing cracks between the tracks inhumed beneath the hill,
then spawned the spores of Grathic wars that profit from the kill;
their victory tales, like crimson crails, reside in dung and dill.

Those scrilly clouds that cowed the crowds neath radiation snapes
left little less than watercress beneath their coffin's drapes;
well, those unborn cannot adorn the pallor of the prapes
for scrundlemun tinged bibberun, wee ones who reaped the
wrapes.

Yes, now-abandoned hetzelspan were once in time embroiled
like merikained that firps enchained until the weather roiled.
What more, perchance, can happenstance inflict upon the koiled
when doves on ships are in eclipse and wrapes of Grath are soiled?

―――――――――――

Retired, Terrance enjoys sitting in the garden with some tea and a
piece of pie thinking about the word and life and all that, trying to
get inspired. Allpoetry.com/loquaciousicity

[S. Libellule]

Watermark

The poeted page is full
of nothingness...

empty words on vacant lines
random thoughts of many kinds

dumped out
all in doubt

it leaves me here spent
left to repent
for every other sin
as tears then douse the spark

to reveal their watermark

Libellule is originally from New England and now lives outside
Birmingham, Alabama. The poet writes about nature,
authenticity, and the examined life. Influences include Mary
Oliver and Billy Collins. Allpoetry.com/Little_Dragonfly

[Casey Renee Kiser]

Ultimately

the depths of the darkest hours
on a daylight quest
the depths of gun barrels laughing
at my bulletproof vest
the depths of Misery, Inc.
tried their very best but
the depths of the ocean [~I]*ultimately*[~IX]
allow my rest

And my rise

the tide rocks me like a mother
Luna sings sweet ~
the stars keep my secrets
and save me a seat
the depths of mental illness once
convinced me of defeat
the depths of the ocean [~I]ultimately[~IX]
will allow me to meet

Ascension

Poem inspired by the song Liquid Diamonds. CRK's poetry
explores identity issues connected with trauma.
Allpoetry.com/i_am_snail_viXen

A Zombie Girl

I'm running, walking, hiking, and searching,
Crossing over highways I haven't seen,
Carrying everything I own on my back,
Looking for home in a dream.

I have to go pee, but bathrooms are broken,
Some of them work but no floors,
Toilets are harder than shit to find,
Some are hidden behind many doors.

I'd stop to play video games there on the street,
One game has a map to my car,
Also a map to a safe house is there,
But it turned out to just be a bar.

Human mannequins without any heads,
Walk about a small space,
The walls are green with mold and disease,
And dangling eyes hit my face

A Zombie girl comes rushing in,
Green as acid with pink hair in curls,
She tells me "You need to wake up from this dream,
Those mannequins used to be girls."

I run and I run until my feet become jelly,
The mannequins gaining on me,
I jump on a train that flies over Africa,
But I lose my grip and start falling.

Then I woke up.

Ragathar the Dragon is a writer from Southern Oregon who is interested in writing her own collection of poetry. She wishes to be a famous author for YA fiction and is currently working on a novel. Allpoetry.com/RagatharTheDragon

[Russell Nailor]

Fractured Finale

Here
In the madness
Of it all
I watch
The angels fall
Sun blotted
From the sky
As I hear
The masses cry
A canticle
For one who's lost
On these plains
Of existence
A requiem
For one who's fought
On the side
Of resistance
Carrying the burdens
Of a
Long forgotten world
As the threads
Of reality
Come unfurled
So many hearts
Bleed

As I sing
My final song
This mortality
I leave
As the fates
Sing along
House
Torn to rubble
Chair
Charred to the floor
No hope
No joy
No love
Lives here anymore
The pursuits of man
Nothing more now
Then a tin can
Corrupted by rust
As they're crushed
To dust
So many souls
Darkened by envy
Darkened by greed
Cut down by four
Riding their mighty
Steeds
So many names
For what
We face now

Could it be
This time
We're not
Making it out
Ragnarok
Apocalypse
Revelations
It's on my lips
What name
What title
Do I give
This point in time
Cursed to wonder here
Though I've
Committed no crime
Stuck with the heathens
You call
Society
I'm nothing
Like them
So why
Still punish
Me.

If not by words, then how does one express themselves? In reality,
I am ordinary. In my dreams, I am extraordinary.
Allpoetry.com/Russell_Nailor

[S. Libellule]

Ashen

Love ignites itself
with a hidden spark
to light the dark
of all our loneliness
how bright it does burn
until we finally learn

how cold is the old grey ash

Libellule is originally from New England and now lives outside Birmingham, Alabama. The poet writes about nature, authenticity, and the examined life. Influences include Mary Oliver and Billy Collins. Allpoetry.com/Little_Dragonfly

[Lisa F. Raines]

Trumpublicans

What has happened to
the Grand Old Party?

How did Ronald Reagan's
reviled "Evil Empire"
become Donald Trump's
"Dictator's Dream Team"?

With faux outrage from
ghosts of the "Tea Party",
we have inherited a
fascination with fascism.

My way or the highway
leaves a lot of people on
the side of the road,
stranded and often forgotten,

taking too many of us
through Gullible's Travels
to the Coup of Fools
and Tools.

———————————

AlisRamie is from North Carolina, USA.
Interests include: philosophy, history, international relations,
poetry, art, design, jazz, funk rock, and some good old soul.
Allpoetry.com/AlisRamie

[Amy Albudri]

Untouched by Seasons' Ravish

Untouched by seasons' ravish
Yet still enthralling.
Lie not awake my heart in mourning
For morning may yet roll the stone away.

Earthy orbs of joy await
But toiled not these tombs;
Since who can touch what not yet blooms
For need of bride within?

The author is composing her first collection of poetry in memory
of a cherished loved one. This verse commemorates the second
anniversary of dear Jasmine's departure.
Allpoetry.com/Handel's_Messiah

[Cliff Turner]

Please, Daddy

Daddy burned the house down
I was in bed when his match was lit
After a night of yelling about it
Frantically pacing
His footsteps booming below my bedroom
His barking shouts
His audible, desperate grin
Making me flinch again and again
Uncontrollable tears
He said he can't handle it anymore
Her memory
Her ghost
It was either him or the house
He came and got me at least
The orange glow is behind us now
I can see it in the side mirror
I cough and cry
I choke
My throat raw with smoke
His eyes raw with emptiness
Please Daddy, please
Keep this car on the road

Cliff writes from Alberta, Canada. Delving into the raw emotions found in dark circumstances, his aim is to give a strong voice to that which is usually whispered. Allpoetry.com/Cliff_Turner

[Brenda Arledge]

No Room for Deceit

He goes through motions
with a hidden agenda up his sleeve,
speaking shady words,
he wants her to believe.

Betrayal cannot touch this queen,
nor stir her emotions dry,
her senses much too keen,
to fall into the pit
of the sneaky trap he's weaved.

This maize of life
weighs heavy on her mind,
watching as the hands on the clock
spin out of time.

There's no wiggle room
for moments of deceit,
only true feelings of attachment
can conquer the feelings
she's buried deep.

―――――――――――――

Brenda Arledge is a poet from Ohio.(United States)
Her poetry is published in numerous publications.
Her poetry is printed regularly in Dimple Times, The Writers
Club -GreyThoughts.info & Hubpages.
Allpoetry.com/Brenda_Arledge

[Marta Green]

Finding Me

knowing as early as the sixth grade
having written notes for girls to say
to the boy of the week
that I would be a writer

adoring letters asking if a girl wanted to go steady
internal pounding destruction for break up notes

by the age of eighteen,
I wanted to have a number one best-selling novel
where did these ideals go? life

it is only now as a young senior citizen
the old appetite to write has risen from the cold and chilly grave
words flowing as natural as a winding, blue green river

don't know where these ideas come from
raining down with monsoon ferocity, inspired, smooth, amazing
watching all types of movies and reading books
Stephen King is my muse now and will be eternally

planning for the future means I will have to put poetry aside
to write short stories for anthologies
take a year to write my first novel

ready to take a leap of faith!
to make people feel deep exhilaration
enjoy comedies, ache for drama stories, on the edge from horror
an author is who I was meant to be

Marta Green is from the state of Texas where she lives with her husband and son. She has a passion for writing poetry and short stories, her family, and animals. Allpoetry.com/Marta_Green

[Jaye Showalter]

Black Valentine

I don't understand how love turns to sand;
how promises bind like twine.
Who could drown in her eyes, her buttery sighs,
my malevolent black valentine.

Too soon I discovered she gave to another
all she had pledged was mine.
The same words and story she first set before me,
repeated line for line.
And he sat before her to dine.
In the web of a black valentine

He thought he could keep her, and so I released her;
surrendered what never was mine.
The faint scent of rose,
the dreams that won't close,
tangled sheets where we once lay entwined,
are all I have left.
The rest has been swept
across ink-stained canyons of time.
To die in the throes of the longing that grows
to be with my black valentine.

––––––––––––––––––

Jaye writes from San Diego, California. Her childrens' poetry book 'Please Pass the Rainbows' was published this year. Allpoetry.com/Jaye_Showalter

[Marcheller Banks]

Hearts of Sorrow

I remember that warm spring afternoon, you called me to say, "my child is missing," then about an hour later you called me back again to say, "she was found." I asked, how was she doing and you told me, "she was with grandma, that of course meant only one thing, she was dead. I couldn't do anything but scream at the time because I was in such disbelief and the sound of your voice confirmed it for me, while the softness of it faded away.

I knew words of comfort wouldn't do any good, because losing your only child would be so hard to endure. There were so many hearts of sorrow that day, especially yours, that I knew at that moment, felt so empty, not really listening to what others had to say. And at the days end, it didn't really matter so much, how she died or why, you just knew you would never see her alive again, say hello or I love you, but yet daily passing an empty room where she used to be.

———————————

I am currently a 61 year old African-American Female. I started writing at the age of 55. I give God all the Honor, Praise and Glory for working through me in this way.
Allpoetry.com/LifeWarrior2000

[George L. Ellison]

The Wheel of Time

The wheel of time
consists of many a spoke
There reside the souls
of many folk

All awaiting
their turn to appear
as beloved souls
to their family so dear

Begetting children
of their own
as the wheel of time
rolls on and on

Each in turn
as in time before
when their time is done
the wheel turns once more

It has been so since the dawn of time
the wheel of fate
bestows unknown periods of life
on all mankind

We come, we go down the ages
ancient ancestors on dusty pages
all reside on the wheel of time
ghostly souls and spirits divine

Awaiting God's call
to inherit a soul
to be the next generation
make a family whole

I have written poetry all my life but mainly since 1994 when I
really started to take it seriously
I have always enjoyed english language and literature
and generally enjoying life as I live it

Allpoetry.com/Queserasera

[Claire O Dwyer]

Memory of my dearest friend

I Remember back to the first day when life had been tough and challenging...

I was dealing with emotions pushing through the pain and in you walked with a smile on your face..

The red sweater you wore not long did you share the warmth of understanding a friend that was rare..

You were there when anxiety struck no words needed to be spoken, our connection so strong never to be broken..

Your red sweater here near me each day to cherish the memories, that smile on your face..

Our friendship will live on forever beyond time and I am happy that you will always be in my life..

Poem about my best friend Cormac. Who will forever have a big space in my heart. Memories I will hold so near, and blessed to have shared. Love Always and miss forever
Allpoetry.com/Claireod

[Jennifer Grant]

Seduced

I was seduced by you,
You were all that consumed my thinking,
The things only you could do to my body,
nobody could do the things you do,
But now I'm sinking,
We were naughty,
Now there's only pain,
My heart is torn,
Into the dark I fall,
Nothing to gain,
I'm nothing but a thorn,
You seduced me and I can't move on.

———————

Jennifer Grant is from Quincy, IL. I help care for the elderly as a dietary aid and I love what I do. Poetry gives me an outlet to express how I feel. Allpoetry.com/Jennifer_Grant

[Carlos Vargas]

Light

You were the light in the darkness who shone through me,
illuminating the deepest parts that lived within me. Light guiding
me through the darkest of nights and through oceans of pitch
black, bursting through dark clouds and through torrents of
storms - conquering those silver linings. That warm unwavering
light, like a hand reaching out to me pulling me through the other
end. There is a loving light that lives within your soul and every
day I get sun kissed by its radiance.

Your light will always shine, even if you don't always see it - it will
rise above the darkness. Always fighting to be seen.

Your light can bend, but it will never break - for it is always
constant.

_____

I was born in Mexico but raised in California my whole life. I'm a
screenwriter, filmmaker, and a dreamer. Naturally, poetry always
came second nature to me, so I wanted to further my mind and
my horizons. Allpoetry.com/Cheerupcharlie

[Catherine Jean Lindsey Towery Sales]

Last year

Last year

In twenty twenty
I lost my mom
But I gain
An Angel
Who got her
Wings

Last Year

I cried I cried
I was so sad
Until I open
My eyes
To my surprise
I gained an
Angel

Last Year

My Mother
Has gone
And said
Goodbye
Don't you cry

Hold your
head
Up high
For now
I know
My mom is
An Angel

Last Year

When mom
Got her wings
I was so sad
My heart was
Broken
Until
I realize
When
I open
My eyes
My mom
Got her wings
This means
Everything

Last Year

On December
Twenty six
Two thousand

And twenty
Mama got
her wings
Today
I can
Sing and
be happy
i Celebrate
today
My mama
memories

Last Year

I cried
I cried
This year
I celebrate
My mamas
life
She made
lots Of
sacrifice
For
all of us
Today
I get to
celebrate
Mamas legacy
Mom got

Her wings
Rest in Peace
Mama
Until we
meet
Again
I will celebrate
Your life
Your legacy
No more
Tears
Only happy ones
Love always
Mom

Catherine Sales former Ed Counselor from Compton
CA.Catherine holds several Master's Degree in
Psychology,Education,Human Behavior,& Education Adm Cred.
Former President PA4C M.H .Advocacy 501C.
Allpoetry.com/Cathysalesmftpoet

[Catherine Jean Lindsey Towery Sales]

Middle Age

Middle Age

An Interesting
Phase
An amazing
Stage
Wouldnt trade
Middle Age
For all the
Silver and
Gold
So what if
You think
Its old
Im not old
You are
young
As you feel
I'm in my
prime
Still
Its Called

Middle Age

Sure
I have
A few aches

And Pain
But just
look
At what
I've gain
Yes
Twenty one
Was lots
Of fun
But I would
Rather be

Middle Age

Than young
and
Dumb
My dirty
thirties
Was quite
An interesting
Phase
And those
Fabulous
forties
i Wouldn't
trade
They were
wake
Up calls

but
I'd rather be

Middle Age

and still
I have a ball
My ferocious
fifties
Yes they
Were great
Yes there were
Lots of pain
and Lots
of aches
Medication
needed
Blood pressure
up
Energy
down
at Times
Felt like
The world
was
Spinning
Around
Its cool
And I'm
Not blue
Glad to

Be here
In my

Middle Age

Today
In my
Sexy sixties
They are
the
best
Somehow,I
Manage to
Pass some
Of life test
I've learned
From some
of
of the
Very best
Been burned
Maybe
A few
But
I have
learned
From them
too
Wouldn't
trade
nothing

For My
journey
my Life
Message
At times
Simply
I was a
mess
Part of
The lesson
I guess
Wonderfully
Made
And Blessed
By the best

Middle Age

is The best
Let me
Share
The best
Is yet
To come

Middle age

Approaching
Seventy
That's
Called the

Golden age
You still
May say
Thats
old age
Ok ,my dear
If that's how
You feel
But how
world
You know
You haven't
begin to live
I Still
call it the
Golden Age
When

Middle Age

Is Come and
gone
And
i should
Be so bless
To see my
Seventies
Im sure
To say
Thank you
Father

for
This day
Thank you
For the
joy
And
happiness
of another day
my Golden Age
Is
The best
Yes the best
Is yet
To come
The
Seventies
Are
Golden years
And I will be
Greatful
If im still
here

Middle Age

I guess
What I'm
Trying
to say
It doesn't
matter

What age
or stage
You are
Bless
At any age
When you
Consider the
Alternatives
Before you
Pass
judgement
On someone
age
Think twice
And
open your eyes
And You may
realize
Its a blessing
To learn
valuable
Lessons and to
Appreciate
The gift of life
Which is truly
A blessing
No matter
The age
No matter the
Stage

Just be sure
You
Give God
the Glory
Give God
some
Praise
For all ages

Middle Age

Youth or
Old Age
And thank
God For life
No matter
The stage
Praise God
always
Especially
For
The Golden years
If you are
Still here
Truly bless
By the best
If you have
Pass the test
Share your
message
Not all your

Mess
Share your
Testimony
To help
others
Pass their
Test

Middle Age

I just love
All the ages
But today

Middle Age

Simply the best

Catherine Sales former Ed Counselor from Compton
CA.Catherine holds several Master's Degree in
Psychology,Education,Human Behavior,& Education Adm Cred.
Former President PA4C M.H .Advocacy 501C.
Allpoetry.com/Cathysalesmftpoet

[Jasmine Nicolas]

To my one and only

Hold me close
Hold me tight
Don't let me go tonight.
Our love is pure
Our love is rare
Let's not throw it away.
Hold the memories close to your heart,
In bed with your favourite t-shirt,
You stare at me like a work of art
and I stare at your lips like it was made for only me.
To my one and only,
I know that someday,
we'll cross paths again
and maybe we'll be good for each other then.

Mother, traveler, poet, & whiskey drinker.
I like creating things and I am usually inspired by new experiences
and discoveries. Allpoetry.com/jasmine.nicolas

[Udo Andre]

A Day in the Life of a Murderer

"Defendant will rise
and hear the verdict
as spoken aloud by the jury."
"Your honor, we find
the defendant is guilty
of murder in first degree."
"So say you one, so say you all?"
"It's murder in first degree."

The words were echoed
throughout the court,
and ground into his brain.
A bolt of shock
crept through his body-
it eases into pain.
A reign of terror, horror, fear-
it eases into pain.

The courtroom explodes
with violent eruption
like that of a volcanic flare.
The gleeful vengeance
of electrical crowds-
is lingering around in the air.
A humid and gagging environment now.
It's lingering around in the air.

The phone booths were filled
with anxious reporters,
all eager to earn salary.
Photographers clawing
and gnawing for pictures,
to add to death row's gallery.
The final trip to infamy-
to death row's gallery.

The news spread out
into the streets.
"I hope they gas the bum."
"What did I say?"
"Too bad." "Two bits!"
"His hell has just begun."
He's endlessly waiting, just waiting for doom.
"His hell has just begun."

The sentence then read,
that "In thirty-five days:
it is death by means of the state."
To die in a chamber
that's reeking of gas-
what a horrid and ominous fate.
It's such an inhuman and cruel punishment.
What a horrid and ominous fate.

He's sweating it through
every day after day,
but now, there's one solution:

"Thank God," says he,
prolonging his fate-
"A stay of execution!"
He's so relieved and breathes again.
A stay of execution.

Yet time is impatient
and it hurries on,
as death prepares its meal.
He's desperately fighting,
and clinging to hope:
he wins another appeal.
The vicious cycle grinds again.
He wins another appeal.

So, on and on
his suffering burns,
Now savoring every breath.
He knows a thing
that few men know:
mere hours before his death.
He knew a thing that few men knew:
eleven years of death.

To accompany him
on that final walk
was death disguised as man.
They dragged him in
and strapped him down.
His final torture began.

A helpless, frightened creature now.
His final torture began.

Like deafening sounds
of atomic bombs:
the tiny package dropped.
His mind screamed.
His body writhed.
His breathing now had stopped.
No more must he endure the pain.
His breathing now had stopped.

"Come on! Wake up!"
He felt a splash,
a chill upon his face.
"Are you alright?"
He felt his head
now swimming a furious pace.
He's unbelieving of his mind,
now swimming a furious pace.

Ecstatic joy!
Rejoice, relief!
"It's all just a terrible dream!"
"You only passed out
when the jury returned.
Quiet down, you are causing a scene."
"Oh, why? What the hell? Hey, where am I now?"
"Quiet down you are causing a scene."

"Defendant will rise
and hear the verdict
as spoken aloud by the jury."
"Your honor, we find
the defendant is guilty
of murder in first degree."
"So say you one, so say you all?"
Repeating eternally...

_____

Born in Germany, raised in Washington state, U.S.A.
For the past few years, I have been writing on Quora, where I am
known as the Lizard of Awes/ Deputy to the Chief Outlaw of the
Bottom Writers. Allpoetry.com/Scrapiron1027

[Deedra Tinsley]

Things Done In Vain

To the things done in vain
Such atrocities are the disdain
How petty of any man is pondered
To have left comfort or wandered
Till nigh instead unrest shall haunt
In manner of loath to taunt
Rested eyes for the weary fiend
Surpassing fire waiting to be careened
Fellow foul want not participate
For undying sadness is sealed by fate

My siblings, my sons, and my parents have the greatest impacto in my writing skill. Truly I thank them the most! With love Miss D
Allpoetry.com/Deedra_Tinsley

[Andrew Lee Joyner]

I see a shadow

There's a figure I see,
Some type of darkness behind me
It's a shadow but it's not mine
A shadow that won't go away

As much as I run, it follows me
The chase becomes a race
A shadow that won't go away

Perhaps it's your shadow, I cannot say
I see the darkness coming my way,
Foggy, musky, bleak
A shadow that won't go away

I tried to hide, but then I see
the shadow here is just another me

When I started writing it became a hobby of mine and now it's
my life, I love to read and write. My inspiration is life, my sister is
my muse Allpoetry.com/Andrew_Lee

[Sean Cooke]

[Life's Carousel]

The world turns with regularity.
Human beings want diversity.
Up, down and round like a carousel.

If you knew the secret to life, would you tell?
The world turns and the winds shift.
We can't keep up with life because we are adrift.
The carousel goes around but it's rusty and weak.

It stops momentarily because something new we seek.
The world turns and we pull away.
We want to keep up but in our comfort zone we stay.
Caught between reality and dreams.

Caught in-between facts and lies.
Seeking answers with the word why.
Caught in-between smiles and cries.

———————

I am a 31 year old man from northern England, reading and writing poetry is now a satisfying and productive part of my life. I thank my mother and father deeply and all those who read my poetry. Allpoetry.com/Arsenalfan30

[Patricia Marie Batteate]

The Power of Words

There are two sides to every story
So let us not be too hasty
Don't wet your pallet with nasty lies
You may find them not so tasty

Don't repeat the things you hear
Out of reckless idle babbling
You could destroy someone's life
A place where you shouldn't be dabbling

Put yourself in someone's shoes
And listen to what is said
Don't entertain one's hunger for hate
Decipher what's feeding your head

Consider the truth at hand
The sincerity of the source
Don't follow the path of hateful fools
You might find you were way off course

Don't be afraid to defend the honor
Step up to the plate and say
If that person were here before you
You wouldn't have the guts to betray

We all have reasons to rant
Don't let it become a habit
Negative energy is harmful
Like the bite of a dog that is rabid

So beware of the town crier
Spreading more lies than facts
Words have a very long shelf life
Somethings you can never take back

———————————

I am a 7th generation Californian. I am an engineer, poet and
artist. 'Tolerance is a gauge used to determine just how much a
person is willing to put up with'

Allpoetry.com/Patricia_Marie

[April Hamlin-Sache]

Then I Say

Looking above at the sky,
I hear the wind blowing
then I say oh my,
the sun is strong and so am I.

I listen to the cars passing by,
I hear the engine roar
then I say oh my.

Rain starts to fall from the sky,
I whisper in my male friend's ear
then I say oh my.

Next, the doorbell begins to ring
in the middle of my song that I sing
then I say oh my.

My ex-boyfriend is at the door
then I say oh my.

It is all in my mind,
I reminisce,
I miss my ex.

We have been apart for years,
I cry, inner tears
I sigh, then I say oh my.

He is gone from my life
but not forgotten,
I wish that I had not ended our dating-ship.

He asks me to remain his friend,
I said no all because
I was fed up with being his girl on the side.

I am originally from Indiana. I have 5 poetry books, 2 books of short stories and 6 series on amazon.com. I am a PT receptionist and a writer. I love what I do! I Luv reading poetry! Allpoetry.com/April_Sache

[Sindy Mitchell]

Song of Spring

The ardent sun spreads its rays over the crystal stream,
The natural world reawakens,
The eastern comma butterfly looms from its cocoon,
Into a rebirth of days to come,
The wind whispers its sweet melody,
As I break the sprigs from the bushes,
The love that was lost in the winter past,
My heart ached in a burning tremor,
With the pounding rain that blinded my tears,
I muddled in disarray,
In the cold, dark night,
Then I saw the blossoming of deciduous magnolias,
With the sweet scent of flavor,
With compassionate eyes,
That held me in a loving embrace,
A renewal of affection surrounded my broken heart,
Hope arose from a deserted abode,
As the thriving bud opens a new life,
Into a world of euphoria,
As the red-winged blackbird warbles a song,
O mother earth, let us glorify our risen souls,
Amidst the rolling hills and exuberant, blossoming daffodils,
Over the old secretive woods with endless grass,
O hear our sweet aria of tenderness and adulation,
In this magnificent song of spring.

Sindy Mitchell enjoys teaching children and playing music. She graduated from the University of Toronto with a science degree and a teaching certificate. She has a Master's degree in Counselling. Allpoetry.com/S._Mitchell

[Jonathan Myers]

Hope

A red sun sets in a silent world
The memories of those once beside you,
fade away into lonely spirits

Others who remain are reduced to lifeless shells,
wandering in circles, searching for a treasure
long forgotten
Their roads lead to a dead end with no return

But you sit with resolve, in an evening robbed of twilight,
for the fire in your heart still burns with life
The path is quiet and devoid of life,
but you still search for that last ray of sunshine

In this land of the wayfaring hollows,
you mark and pen your very own map
Through onyx crags with no light in sight,
determination will ignite your torch
Broken and beaten by doubt and despair,
hope may mend your beaten soul

The abyss is oppressive,
like a night that never ends,
but the sun will shine again in reward for the brave and resilient

Your journey may be lonesome,
and the pathways quiet and empty,
but you walk with the footsteps of
like-minded warriors
Even in a world of perpetual darkness,
you are NEVER alone

I was raised in Daleville, Indiana. I turned to poetry in the last few years as a way to give a voice to the heavy echoes of the heart. Allpoetry.com/John_Quinten

[Isabella Si-On Smarro]

Boy On Fire

There once was a boy
who [~I]*fell*[~IX]°•°•°•°~

Not in love,
nor into regret.
But just simply against the ground.

His poor scratched face,
Fit within the cracks-
Of the pallet wood.

Inch length pieces,
cradle against the waves-
-Of his cheeks.

While all
He does
Is cry.

Perched lips
Crackle to
The stinging
Of splinters-

-Silence fills
In the gaps
Between°~

The birthing
Of a tear
And when
It hits
The ground.

That empty second
Filled with agony and desire
Lits something [~I]*dangerous*[~IX] inside.

Pounding
Upon the now broken heart-
-A flame is [~I]*made*[~IX]!

No emotional
Guidance is
Given-

-So the already unpredictable
Boy becomes a monster,
Who without
A second
Thought~

~sets fire
To the [~I]*world*[~IX]

The only
Hope given
Is the water within the wood
That the poor boy once cried...

Isabella is a student at Hudson Valley Community College who loves to write poetry. She's been published in books, newspapers, and magazines. Allpoetry.com/Paralyzed_Fox

[Lonna Lewis Blodgett]

Sand on the Shore of Stars

We follow light
To come out of the darkness
We enter darkness
To hide from the light
We are the dawn and the dusk
We are the fathoms of grey
That stand like shadows in-between
The place of mourning
And joy of love
Composing frontiers of never knowing
From where we have come
To ultimately find our peace
Our only solace
Is in the grain of sand
On the beaches of eternity
In the cosmos of our being
Searching for God

I have spent a lifetime searching for answers regarding truth and meaning. I have found in the art of poetry the uniqueness of intrinsic language as the conveyance of the human experience. Allpoetry.com/Lonna_Blodgett

[S. Libellule]

Unpenned

It is the very words
you cannot write

which will forever haunt

Libellule is originally from New England and now lives outside Birmingham, Alabama. The poet writes about nature, authenticity, and the examined life. Influences include Mary Oliver and Billy Collins. Allpoetry.com/Little_Dragonfly

[Ashley Evans]

The Yearning Eagle

He hears a distant call in the far sun-kissed horizons,
pleading for Him to venture south.
It soon came to be that his journey
led Him there, an unfamiliar route.

What strange and unforgiving land this was
in turning sweet joys to imminent danger.
His golden wings carried Him further still,
all caused by the voice of a stranger.

The quest to find the Source took five years
of circling the chaotic land below,
resulting in the yearning of the wise predator
and simply needing to know.

Who did this siren's call belonged to
and will He ever find Her here?
Soon, it called to Him again,
as a love song oh so near.

Ashley is from Milton, FL and enjoys miniature painting and
writing poetry in her spare time. She also enjoys spending time
with friends and family, cooking, and reading.
Allpoetry.com/Aquanite16

[Heather Porterfield Palmer]

In the Sun

Yes My hand runs along the stiff, textured screening
My fingertips softly palpate the cold black vinyl
The unlit red button momentarily glows scarlet,
Caught in a ray of sunlight through the blind

The dank aroma of old smoke and laughter
Fills the cold, quiet air of the cluttered studio
Phil's ghost sits silently ahead of me
With that sinister cigarette stuck in his bass strings

A full set stands unceremoniously in the corner
The tom is beat all to hell, I trace it with an index finger
A melancholy tear slips down my cheek for Kevin
I smile, closing my eyes

I was young, thin, and gorgeous
Vivaciously owning the stage, roaring, and
My guys behind me, smiling and steady
The music loud, full of pain, power, and resolve

Blessed gifts, God-given and abundant,
Lavished upon us, poured out through us
Until the stage transformed
A tabernacle; perspiration, our offering

My father's fingers raced over his strings, confidence his gasoline
Brimming with sage wisdom, yet the zest of youth
The bass was a plane ascending, the vibration
Riveting stage and soul

The drums, the fat heartbeat of an old washer
Formidable, steady
Tony's keyboard, quiet blue eyes and fiery hands
It was perfect, and we knew it

The magic was finally scattered, as magic always is
For it refuses to be contained in mortal bodies
In vintage amplifiers or stale microphones
In faded lyrics scribbled upon yellowed paper

Time has pounced now, a bastard scoundrel
My voice is stalwart, an elixir in a weathered vial
More seldomly taken or opened, so that soon,
Might none drink my beautiful antidote?

My brothers in this peculiar worship, whisked away
Only distant echoes remain of former joys and triumphs
It was our moment in the sun, I muse,
As the ray of sun leaves the red button, and it dulls

Heather is a Northeast Texas native. She is wife, mother of six,
grandmother, vocalist, lactation and health professional, and a
writer. 'I write to survive life as an empath.'
Allpoetry.com/H74soul

[Marisol Rodriguez]

Mother's Love Never Ends

A Mother's love never ends
It's truly miraculous you know
To me she was like the Blessed Mother
Who was by his side to his end

My mother often said I want to go first
I can not be like your Godmother Hilda
Now I know what she meant by that
My aunt buried her husband son and two daughters

She is called by many the Matriarch
So she only has grandchildren left
Even the Pandemic has taken many
But her faith never failed her

My mother on the other hand had four
But in reality she had over a hundred
She adopted many many friends of ours
For they all called her mom till the end

She was an inspiration to many who knew her
She was always lending a helping hand
I was raised to take on that goodness
Which I have been abiding since she told me

My fiancée says you have a heart of gold
If I did I'd be a millionaire's
Thinking what to say to everyone
Well it's not easy and you never forget

You find her in the sun moon the stars
The very air you breathe indeed
You probably are saying the aroma
Yes when you first step into her house

The lingering smells of her home
Like the Vanilla Lavender candles she liked
That she made me only buy them for every occasion
But most of all I miss the way she called me

To check on me when I slept over with her
My breakfast was ready we prayed ate and out
To her favorite place we went once in a while
The casinos to ching a ling as she she called it

I will always treasure the times kandi and me, Spent playing
pokeno
Oh of course my brother David too
But how she would win and kandi as well

They had competition who wins coverall
Now it's time to say not goodbye
But till we meet again I love and miss you Mami
Remember that a Mother's love never ends

I love life and poetry.

I am simply Me Marisol

I am engaged to fellow Poet Vince O'Neill since 2015

Proud mother of 8 Pete, Carlos , Alexander , Benjamin , David ,
Angel , Mariah and Nalina Allpoetry.com/SimplyMeMarisol

[Lisa F. Raines]

Ruts over roots

Buried paths
Forming over years with
Sweat, love and hard work

Deformed and deforming
Conforming to a certain
Growth and depth and
Hardening over the years

Roots entwine
Crushing weight
Forcing directions and
Changing opportunities

Genetic factors
Environmental influences
Balance causes in
Personal expression

AlisRamie is from North Carolina, USA.
Interests include: philosophy, history, international relations,
poetry, art, design, jazz, funk rock, and some good old soul.
Allpoetry.com/AlisRamie

[Lisa F. Raines]

Stop "Peace for our time"

Appeasement
does not save us
from the next war

Will "spheres of influence"
bring us a bipolar world?
More stable? but never safe

A Cold War, a hot war
Will we leave it to the
"little green men"?

Is Ukraine Putin's
Czechoslovakia?
Crimea, his Sudetenland?

Hitler had no
compunctions about
breaking every pact

Does Vladimir Putin?

AlisRamie is from North Carolina, USA.
Interests include: philosophy, history, international relations,
poetry, art, design, jazz, funk rock, and some good old soul.
Allpoetry.com/AlisRamie

[S. Libellule]

Inky

So
black
ever thick

ink ever slick

claims my page

douses a deep rage

in its own soothing way

watching it further spread

across the surrendering page

while the words ride a poetic flow

this lonely poet seems able to know

poetry

Libellule is originally from New England and now lives outside Birmingham, Alabama. The poet writes about nature, authenticity, and the examined life. Influences include Mary Oliver and Billy Collins. Allpoetry.com/Little_Dragonfly

[Fadwa Saidani]

Sober

I am no longer sober
One day I'm on top the world
Tomorrow I'm a sleepless night,
a 3 a.m thought,
a teardrop of snow,
and void of every word.
All I consumed
Is consuming me still.
All that I loved
Waves in a mortal sea.

No amount of words
Can detach me from reality
day by day
I'm not what I'll become
not what I'm supposed to be.
Today I am what you used to see.
Thought my past agony
will welcome me
with open arms
but my eyes are missing their glow,
and my mind is a soldier without arms.

I am no longer sober.
I won't recover
for I know all around me

is deluded
and what I feel
have never been more real.
I'm walking
to eternal melancholy.

Fadwa Saidani is a Tunisian aspiring poet who studied a master's in cross-cultural poetics. She has been writing poetry for 8 years and she is currently working on publishing her first book. Allpoetry.com/Fadwa_Saidani

[Pete Erlandsen Jr.]

Stare

You are so captivating that I find myself staring at you.

I see you not as an object of lustful gratification, but rather the muse of a priceless work of art.

Your presence is a magnificent masterpiece of beauty, spirituality, and depth.

You are all that I desire, complete and perfect.

Life well lived! I grew up all over, and have experienced much first hand. I've made mistakes and masterpieces. I'm just your average person. Allpoetry.com/Prerlandsen

[Kylie R. Fothergill]

The Sea of Darkness

I am empty.

A conquered carcass in a vast sea of ash.

I am singed.

A forever reminder of the end of someone's lash.

I am lonely.

For I am afloat, alone in the sea.

I am cold.

Yet I'm burning where they can't see.

I am bored.

Tired of the same old sky.

I am wet.

Drenched from the tears I've cried.

Because I am cold,

With a heart that still bleeds,

And I am lonely.

For no one cares but for their greed.

I am singed.

Forever a drift of slumber's sorrow,

And I am empty.

Forever awaiting the light of tomorrow,

But I am understanding

And know it will never come to save me.

For I am accepting

In knowing that they can't see what I see.

In the end,

I am the sorrow throughout history.
I speak for them.
I hold their constant misery.
I am alone.
For I am the only one that can share
The knowledge of knowing
That the weight of the world is hard to bare.

The darkness we feel in our hearts is difficult to express. Allow me
to try and share what I have learned the best.
Allpoetry.com/Thepoetoftheages

[Nicole Jean Baptiste]

Learning to love

A girl with a heart that's been shattered many time,
No love in this world she's lost and alone,
Getting her hopes up messing around,
Everyone she meets could never understand,
Living her life is like being in hell she's learning to love,
In this sinful world crying for help,
No one but her can feel all this pain,
Endless tears fall down her face
she's all alone learning
to love.

Just trying to find me. Been lost in this world for quite some time
now. Words are my freedom, the ink is my pain bleeding on the
canvas. Allpoetry.com/hearts_of_gold

[Jared Griffith]

A Lovers Worth

What is your worth you may ask?
Measuring is no simple task.
It's not really a number that is easy to see.
More of actions or the lack of them if you please.

We all hope that ours will tip the scale.
But for me it is misery and hell.
I want to be special to have worth and pride.
The results came in and I just want to hide.

I want to get the marks that I gave to you.
The results I'm seeing just can't be true.
I've tried so hard, spent every last dime.
The ticket reads better luck next time.

There you have it so plain and simple to see.
No one will ever see my worth, I guess only me.
It's hard when you have given everything you have.
In the end you never mattered, it's all quite sad.

Those tears, fears and worries you went through.
Just the down payment of a future with out you.
I don't want to live and I don't want to hurt.
I'm ready to be done and lay under some dirt.

I fought hard I did everything I could I thought I did it all!
In the end my worth, I wasn't even worth a simple call.
Not sure how I'll do it this time.
Rest assured for me it is the end of the line.

I guess I needed more than you were willing to give.
To be honest since you told me I wasn't worth the gifts I didn't
want to live.

Yes when I measure my worth compared to what I was doing for
you.
I'm working in negative numbers now but I was the glue.
When his leg was hurt I saw you leave with a purpose and in a
rush.
Your words echoed I let him down he needed me so much.

I've needed you many times begged for you but all I got was a
nope.
That's when you left me hanging from the end of a rope.
I've been through a lot, there is much I didn't tell.
Doesn't matter I'll explain it in hell.

Jared Griffith is from Idaho. While enjoy all the grandeur of the West. He fills his thoughts with being the hopeless Romantic that he is. Allpoetry.com/Jared_Griffith

[Jared Griffith]

Two Dragonflies

Two dragonflies move across the water wings beating fast, one
afraid to move forward because of the past.
One flying as fast as it can, excitedly flying toward this
relationship that will last.
Somehow they fly together wings closer and closer to each other.
One will slow down and wait for its lover.
The other will speed up gradually shedding the fear it used as
cover.
Together they will fly together forever in love with one another.

For Lisa Coles

Jared Griffith is from Idaho. While enjoying all the grandeur of
the West. He fills his thoughts with being the hopeless Romantic
that he is. Allpoetry.com/Jared_Griffith

[Tracie Campanella]

My Best Friend

I hurt my bestfriend today,
I really hurt her bad, I have
no one to blame, but myself.
I hurt myself today
I focus on the pain
The only that's real...
The pain in hurting you
is far more intense than
any pain I ever felt in my life.
I was crying last night, like every night
I cry myself to sleep.
Heart broken that I could
hurt my bestfriend the way I did.
We may not be friends,
I hope not enemies,
Just strangers with
some memories.
I'm sorry for hurting you.
I never want you to feel
bad in any way.
It was childish of me,
and I don't expect you to
forgive me.
I just want you to know I'm sorry.
I'm sorry wasn't honest with you,

I'm sorry I made mistakes,
I still care for you I always will.
I found my soul sister
the day we met.
I thought nothing could
tear us apart, but
something did.
It wasn't you, it was all me,
My selfishness, not being
honest with the one person
who was always there.
I'm truly sorry for hurting
you my bestfriend.
If I could see you one more time,
To let you know how much you
mean to me, would be the most
meaningful moment of my life.
I care, and love, and never forget
The wonderful caring person you are.
I hope one day we can be
friends again.
Until that day comes
I cherish the memories we
had made, the laughter, the
silliness, and all your great
advice.
I will always love you
for the great person
you are

I wrote this poem for my best friend, it was my way to apologize for hurting her. I never meant to hurt her the way I did, I hope and pray that we can be friends again. I miss all the fun that we had Allpoetry.com/Tlcampanella19

[Steve Dupere]

From out of Perfection

A womb sets free its keep, a mother her sense of obligation, brought forward to a calling, sharpened fast before he who bore legs left to carry his cross into a flame of doubt and fear where life assures but redundant days and nights.

Child gazes from belly hard into worm-eaten earth, born as a diamond into perfection, broken into dysfunction of sediment and learned living.

The fetus who bears innate love drifts in fullness of yet unobtained knowing; It feels not as it sees a sun which soothes the chill of cold but scorches wisdom of seeing men and that it reaps but the burn of innocence and naivete'.

The child sees from an eye of sinlessness and absolution able to discern, for it is of virtue and purity.

Nurtured are the fertile like keen biddings time hastens to meld as a fleck of knowing and maturation of all man's sin; the grandeur of what is known be a pinnacle far too vivid for closed mind to rectify.

Gained is acumen which disperses like seasoned cattail into err of human emotion supplanted as nourishment to Earth and Her fertile need.

Fragmented lay token man as spoil to his inborn journey learn'ed as a
calling of flighted dust from melody to harmony borrowed by wind as an offering of love beholden to a boundless sea of truth, knowledge and understanding...

Steve has been writing poetry since 1998. His book, Waltz of Semantic Tongues, is available on blurb.
Allpoetry.com/Symmetry59

[Lorri Ventura]

God

Tears coursed down his cheeks

As he gazed at the remains

Of what once was Earth

Lorri Ventura is a retired special education administrator living in Massachusetts. Her writing has been featured in a number of anthologies. Allpoetry.com/Lorri_Ventura

[Deidra L. Hubay]

American Apathy

My hands are clean,
I washed them in my kitchen sink.

I didn't hear their screams,
I was listening to an interview with my favorite sports teams.

I didn't see their agony,
I was sitting on the couch playing Xbox on my TV.

I don't feel badly,
It happened halfway around the world from me.

My hands are clean,
I washed them in my kitchen sink.

———————————

Deidra (Dee) Hubay is a Marine Corps veteran, civic organizer, social advocate, and lifelong learner from Pittsburgh, Pa. Allpoetry.com/Deidrahubay

[Denyse Augustitus]

[I remember being little and wanting to

grow up fast]

I remember being little and wanting to grow up fast
Always wishing and praying childhood wouldn't last
Now that i am older i wish i was a kid
So i could have the chance to do things i never did
You take things for granted and the days pass to months and years
Uncertainty of how much time you have left on earth is your
newest fear
The aches and pains and heartache the silver in your hair
The little child you were once is no longer there
While you're young enjoy it for as long as you can
Because before you know it you are an old lady or old man

Originally from New York, I found my way to Pennsylvania. I did
not have a happy childhood or a happy adulthood until I met my
wonderful husband George. It only took 44 years to meet him!
Allpoetry.com/Denyse_Marie

[Jennifer Ramirez]

Dare I

Can passion be anything other
than ephemeral reverie
or is ardor to be forever known
as the antithesis of prodigy?

Lucid silence borne from
the dearth of appetite.
How untroubled a life can be
without the bombastic turn of love.

Bizarre the axiom is that
we would give up
so much brilliance for
one pearl of desire.

And yet, bearing witness to
this malady does nothing
to quiet the delicate longing.

My fasting soul cries out for
a specimen of beautiful disaster.
Dare I feed that fascinating inferno
or is uncomplicated prosperity enough?

———————————

Jennifer is from the pacific island of Saipan. When she isn't drawing or writing, she can be found riding her motorcycle in Nevada. Allpoetry.com/J.L._Ramirez

[Andrej Bugarinović]

Winter's embrace

Another December has come, darling,
but, this time my steps are lonely.
You suddenly left me, my little bird,
flying away to a warmer place.
If you could hear my words - if only!

Do you remember our tree
on which we engraved our names to eternity?
My fingers slide over the rugged letters.
Your slender figure is all I see
in the snowflakes falling ever obliquely.

Do you remember how confused we were
when our lips touched for the first time?
how naively we thought of everything?
how to your soft ears I whispered
my sweetest words, my sharpest rhymes?

Do you remember our kisses
and all the dreams and thoughts we shared
while lying right below the branches?
Those were the white nights of blisses.
Now all I feel is winter's embrace.

Wherever you are, my darling,
I hope one day you walk next to our tree

and feel in your chest an ancient trace
of the person with whom you used to be.
But all I feel is winter's embrace.

Andrej is a medicine student from Bosnia and Herzegovina. He
loves poetry and began writing at the age of fourteen. Life for him
is a huge library in which he finds the inspiration for his works.
Allpoetry.com/Andrjuška

[Jack G Hansen]

Hang in There, Kid

I'm waiting
For the fight
Fantasizing
My victory

Although
Defeat
May be my fate

I'm waiting
For the fight
My fight
That fight

My heroic crescendo
To be a man complete

I'm waiting- I'm waiting

My appearance may be broken
My effort exhausted

But my soul
Remembers
The fight

I have not lost it.

Jack G Hansen resides in Oconomowoc, WI. He is a graduate student, at Southern New Hampshire University.
Allpoetry.com/Gregory_Plum_Society

[Priscilla Ellington]

The Rose Without Petals

There was a rose that lived in a garden,
She did not know what others saw in her,
She'd never seen herself before,
The sun gave light to her,
And the rain soaked into her roots,
And she was happy.

Others would see the rose and admire her beauty,
And they would touch the rose,
But the world was not kind,
Over time she began to lose her petals,
The snow, the wind, and the rain...
had become unkind to the rose,

One by one, her petals fell to the ground,
And one by one, thorns protruded from her stem,
The seasons changed,
and the rose sought to feel joy,
in the sun and in the wind again,

And so the rose would wait.

Days turned into weeks,
and the wind would blow,
and a petal would fall,

Weeks turned into months, and the rose lost more.
As the months turned into a year,
the rose had only one petal left.

One day the sun shined brightly onto the rose,
The rose, once beautiful and full of petals,
thought to give what remained of herself to the sun.

And so she did.
She gave herself to the sun,
For the sun warmed her,
and gave her hope that even in all that she lost,
There would still be light,
and the sun would come back to her each day.

And the sun came back,
day after day,
and shined its rays on the rose,

And she was happy.

From Waxhachie, Texas
Priscilla enjoys painting, and spending time with her dogs in her
spare time. Allpoetry.com/Priscillaellington

[Tim Cedillo Jr]

Dark Days

Gray clouds on the horizon.
the storms move in on an overcast sky.
It simply reminds me of those days i was high.
Everything would be sunny for a minute,
only to be clouded back up.

It doesn't matter how bright your sun is,
those gray clouds are too thick for it to shine through.
Funny how condensation particles cover up a sun thats so bright
it turns the day into dusk.

I had polluted my mind so much i couldnt see the light in
anything.
All my days had turned into night,
as if all hope for me had faded off into oblivion.
Never to return again,
those were the loneliest days of my existence.

i had become a stranger to myself. not knowing who this guy was
looking back at me,
when i looked into the mirror.
would i ever know him?

who are you?
i would ask myself,
as i would plunge synthetic misery into my veins.

In search of something i thought was missing. Each time i would lose that much more of my being,drifting further and further from sanity.

who could love you id tell myself,
and i believed it more and more when i said it each time.
I had become disgusted with myself.

The only love i had for anything came in form of poison.
which i would filter thru cotton,
and sometimes search the tracks for hours on my way to feel happy.

You're such a piece of shit!
i would tell myself,
as my mind would go numb.
I unknowingly became my own worst enemy, hating each breath i took.
Would i ever find what I'm looking for,
or is it my destiny to be miserable for the rest of my days?

i had become irrational in my thinking,
and my delusions only got worse,
as i drifted closer and closer to insanity.

all i could think about is how i had got here to begin with.
I would take another dose of courage so i could begin my journey.
Only to realize i was chained,
in a dungeon so dark i couldn't see myself.

Looking back at those days dont depress me. They dont make me sad,
and im not ashamed.
To be ashamed of it,
would be to be ashamed of Gods work.
Some things are meant to be in life.

Some caves must be explored.
They are dark,
and until you shine a light.
You can't see the beauty or the life thats in it. But it's always been there.
hidden out of sight,
and some of us get lost in the dark.

I thank God today for letting me get lost.
If I hadn't been so lost,
I would've never got to find myself.

From Williamsburg, Ky, Tim has used poetry to help him overcome addiction, and the problems that come along with it. He has came a long way in his recovery proving words truly are powerful. Allpoetry.com/Tim_Cedillo_Jr.

[Tim Cedillo Jr]

A fathers struggle

His heart is calloused and on his sleeve.
He comes home she tells him to leave.
He says I'm sorry I really wanna quit this time.
But she doesn't know he wants to die.
The choice has left him.
Now he can't control his life.
So he drifts even deeper.
He tries to hide what he's doing.
Because he knows it isn't right.
He's so ashamed he wishes that he could quit. He always thinks
how did his life get like this.
He's always struggled,
all he's ever known is pain.
He just thought,
that he was to far gone to change.
He really loved her,
he didn't love the drugs more.
I know the way it looks,
but he never really had a choice.
It's hard to choose when you're an addict.
People don't understand.
They talk down to you,
because they think you are a lesser man.
He never once wanted this to be his life.
He lost his family,

not because he didn't wanna try.

He was consumed by the evil that he didn't see. It destroyed him, his family was his everything.

He knows now that the mistakes were his own. The fault was his now his mind will forever roam. He once had everything now it's all gone.

He doesn't see his kids.

He barely talks to them on the phone.

Not because that's the way he wants it to be.

He might not understand it yet,

but one day he'll see.

The good in all of this.

He takes it day to day.

It's the hardest thing that he's ever done.

He's getting better,

but the battles never gonna be done.

He wants so bad to be a father,

to his daughter and son.

To be the dad they deserve him to be.

He's no good to em high,

and this he sees.

But the time that he's lost is his misery.

It's like the mountain that he's climbing,

goes straight up.

Just so happens that all the pain he's had,

has made him tough.

He keeps climbing he's never gonna give up.

He made bad decisions but that's in the past.

He's working hard so he can get his life back.

So he can smile,

and show his kids the right path.

that no matter how bad your getting beat,

you can fight back.

He'll show them courage,

and what it really means to live.

That you can beat the odds.

Look your dad did.

Keep your head up.

Keep moving no matter how bad it gets.

Maybe one day,

he can be a better dad than this.

But he loves you,

and he's sorry for all the times he's missed.

From Williamsburg, Ky, Tim has used poetry to help him overcome addiction, and the problems that come along with it. He has came a long way in his recovery proving words truly are powerful. Allpoetry.com/Tim_Cedillo_Jr.

[Tim Cedillo Jr]

The beautiful curse

When will it end.
The misery of this moment.
It possessed me like a demonic spirit on a human soul.
Terrorizing my every move.
But those moves weren't mine.
They were driven by taste.
Like a shark on blood.
My mind was corrupted by an obsession.
That was so great nothing would keep me from it.
I was so sick.
There isn't any cure.
I'm forever tainted by its possession.
My stomach hungers for one more taste.
I must refrain from quenching this undeniable thirst.
The demons on my back tempted me at every turn.
My thoughts were poisonous.
I would burn everything down on the way out.
Delusional in a state of psychosis.
I wouldn't know what was real,
And what was fictional.
All just to numb my mind.
I wanted it all to go away.
This demon had sunk it's fangs in me.
In the form of crystals in a baggie,
And liquid in a syringe.
I had never been so hopeless as I was then.

The voices constantly drove me mad.
I still hear them today.
Shadows passing by the trees.
Just waiting to take me away.
I'd never been so haunted in my life
Nothing could have prepared me for the dark road I had turned
on to.
But this was my life.
I had spent hours with blood trickling down my body.
My veins were so thirsty for the poison.
My mind delusional to the pain it was causing me.
I was sure it was the answer to everything.
I never realized the damage,
that would be left in it's aftermath.
I thought for sure I was lost forever.
I once again started over with nothing.
Isn't that what we do.

I'm determined to regain it all.
For once in my life.
I'm not driven by the demon on my back.
Yes I have an uncurable disease.
But I refuse to be a statistic and give in.
Temptation will always be there.
But as long as I have breath in my body.
I have a chance.
I am an addict.
I will go to any lengths to get what I want.
It's a beautiful curse.

From Williamsburg, Ky, Tim has used poetry to help him overcome addiction, and the problems that come along with it. He has came a long way in his recovery proving words truly are powerful. Allpoetry.com/Tim_Cedillo_Jr.

[Emma Steere]

I'm Free

Sometimes life isn't what you think it is going to be.
In the end, all I really needed was me.

A vision planted in my brain,
Long ago, still prevails.

There is no life navigation,
And there are several different,
Transformations.

Hear my words, for I might enlighten you.
My message here is genuine.
This is me,
And thankfully,
I believe I am precisely where I need to be.

I got so lost,
Forgot my way,
But I'm still here today.

Quiet the storm,
mellow the rage,
take a load off your mind,
and hear what I'm about to say.

Set your mind at ease,
And please,
Listen to my story.

Time was wasted,
Offspring draw breath, to be omitted.
For if it weren't for them,
I never would have made it.

Don't be afraid to reveal what you can do.
RAWR back if you must,
Protect and represent,
And be a shield.
It's hard to believe,
But you must see,
Complex situations can happen to anyone,
And everyone, including me.

Soul fire burning,
Changes need made,
Shake things up,
Something inside me has changed.

I still know some souls without hope,
Young, old, abused, abandoned, and broken.
Together now,
Let's Raise the sound.

You gotta live as yourself,
Exactly the way you are.

Let the smoldering flames,
Pierce through.

I'm alive; I'm alive
My heart is still healing,
While struggling to rebuild,
And align for the new.

Dance, Dream, Thrive,
this is your opportunity,
Build your life to be extraordinary.

It is time now,
For you, to treat you better.
Tell me,
What is it that you want to do?

Don't be afraid of this feeling inside,
You are free now,
So, who are you?

Before you answer, let me say
You are strong inside,
And if you crack,
It's ok.

You are allowed to be vulnerable.
Let it out, grant the tears to fall.
Cry, sob, groan, or Howl,
No one can tell you, no now.

You don't have to make everything right,
Be so unsure, always striving to be polite.
I know you learned to always apologize,
Feeling contrite.
Often questioning your sanity,
And doubting your memories.
It's not your fault,
That's called gaslight.

Focus on you and your chickpeas,
And you will achieve great success,
You don't always have to please.

Have some fun just for you,
Then, think about what it is in this life,
That you would actually like to do.

Something unique,
You'll make it,
For you are a Super Star.
Keep moving forward,
No matter what they say.
Hold your head up,
You are excellent and true,
The word might even be "perfect",
Because, you're perfect for you.

I know you'll go far,
For your dreams and goals,

Have never left your mind.
You have plenty of ambition.

We are all beautiful in our own way,
So keep in mind,
Have zero regret for who you are,
Always Love and admire yourself,
Speak your truth,
With sincerity.

When mistakes are made,
There's a moment in time,
I may wander because I feel weak.
I know it can be hard to believe,
But, The sun will shimmer,
And you will be just fine!

Running for way too long,
It's time to be independent and free.
My heart's been asking, "what's my motivation?"
Well, let's take a glimpse, shall we?

Families are torn, a step from the edge,
Another war, losing faith,
Unheard voices,
asking to be saved from the hate,
From the hurt.

People on the verge of giving up,
Defeated,

No longer, are they believing.
They have fear of being alone,
Everything goes black,
About to detonate.

We must stay alive,
as adaptation has past.
Survive the game

The risk of wasting time,
Is keeping me convinced,
I'm here, for the
Battle cries

I'm not a hero,
But a soldier of sort,
Forming together a troop,
To help those,
That have been burnt.

Desire, heart, and fate,
Together make,
The spark,
that creates a team that will shine.

The Misunderstood, used, mistreated, and mistaken,
The underestimated,
or those with so much hatred.

Felt like your nothing,
Filled with guilt and anxiousness,

Left with no choice but to run away,
Due to the Intimidation.
This is not defeat; I have a whole lot left.

Everything matters,
I'm not pretending anymore,
No longer covering,
The untruths,
The abuse.

I'm free to be me, I'm still here.
I now know,
My mind is sound,
I should have never questioned my own intuition.
I no longer need someone's validation.

I felt worthless and all alone,
Periodically, almost lost my will to rebel.
Unable to break me,
You strived even harder for lengths of time,
I told myself "you'll survive,"
I just had to believe.

Just imagine a life,
Not always watching the door,
Worrying, will he be coming back for more?

Although I am damaged,
I have experimented with what I am made of,
And who I am created to be,

And it isn't who you wanted me to be,
You may have held me down,
But I got up.

I know I'll make it out breathing,
And that's more than I could say before.
Don't listen to the hate,
You, were born to fly!

It will forever be an uphill battle,
It's more difficult,
When leaving what you know.
I see the glow, at the end of the tunnel,
Believing in my strength with every step.

Take off your shoes, relax,
Reconnect and visit old friends,
No more isolation.
Fresh air, done carrying that load.

Raise your glass,
For freedom, independence, and liberty.
I'm beginning again.
I'm Free*

Now, My Destiny
Help those in trouble,
The ones who need to assign fault on me.
When scared and mad,
I'll allow em', to take it out on me.

We will take it slow,
You can count on me,
Always Remember, you are filled of beauty.

Your feeling sorrowful and all alone,
And no one seems to care,
I'll be here.
Telling you to hold on,
It gets better than you know.

I spent so many years,
Learning how to survive.

I'm still alive

Let life begin again,
I had a heavy heart,
but no one could hold me back.

Hold your head up,
and tell yourself there is something more,

AND WALK OUT THAT DOOR

-----I'M FREE-----

———————————

Renowned chaos coordinator. Mom of 4, step mom of 3. Past Trauma. Attending college and General Manager of an outdoor Whitewater/ Fly Fishing company.
Allpoetry.com/Chaos_Coordinator

[Margaret Chinyere offoha]

Hope

HOPE, WE MUST HAVE
When the ground around us is shaking.
We must keep hope alive.
When all we have is lost
We must keep hope alive
For hope is like the air we breathe
Hope is like water for a thirsty mouth
Hope is like rain at the end of a drought
Hope is like freedom at the end of captivity
Hope is like food for a hungry stomach
Hope is like tomorrow, for it brings forth the sunrise.
Hope is like the sight of a mother for a child
Hope is like the sight of a father for a child
Hope is like the sight of a sister, brother, friend, and all the people
we love
Hope is like a victory at the end of a war.
Hope is like a beautiful bride walking towards her groom,
Yes, it is the sight of a groom running towards his bride
Hope is the light at the end of a tunnel
Hope is the laughter that will come tomorrow.
Yes, hope we must hold unto
For without hope, we all perish in despair.

Margaret Offoha is from Nigeria, a mother of six. A nurse by
profession. She recently discovered the joy, satisfaction, and
calmness in reading and writing.Allpoetry.com/Margaret_Offoha

[Landen McNiven]

Mom Made The Manna

Mom made the manna,
Her favorite dish,
So her children in the desert would not perish,

Mom made the manna,
So we could know,
She watches us as we learn below,

Mom made the manna,
White as snow,
So we could remember our old home,

Mom made the manna,
To taste so pure,
To remind us her love is the cure

Landen McNiven is from Billings, MT. He loves to create all forms of art. This is the first of many art pieces to come. <3
Allpoetry.com/Landen

[Eric McChesney]

Moonlight Festivities

At a critical stage of life, one must choose a path that best fits their
soul
Circling the keg of joy, I am at that crucial point, dive in or walk
away?
Scanning the beach, eyes wide, I see the path that I would like to
follow
The joyous feeling of a pounding bass and electronic noise, lights
up!

Strolling along the shore, waves crashing at my feet, pondering the
future
A warm wind rustles my hair, smell of salt in the air, the night is
perfect
If it is all falling into place, why do I ponder joining in on the
festivities?
Taking a look out towards the Atlantic, I sense a destination, a
calling

The chaotic scene behind me, a gathering of like minds, same
choices
Turning around, I make my way back to the celebration at hand
Stepping into the glow of the bon-fire, taking in the warmth of
the light
I have made a critical move in the fight for the soul, a split-
decision

Time makes the lovers feel as if they belong, a feeling of togetherness
Feeling the gravity of the music, the smell of the fire, the moonlight
I know what has to occur, live life, enjoy the moment, exist in the world
Sparks flying, music playing, I jump in full boar and live the life...

―――――――――――――

Hailing from Ocean, New Jersey, Eric enjoys spending time with his family and baseball. Poetry is a release that allows for expression and creativity. Allpoetry.com/The_Enigma

[Sandra Avellani]

Five

One. As years of desire culminate at this moment, freedom is the only way to describe it—a want, a need. No binding rules, responsibilities, nor worries. No unfulfilled fantasies or dreams, just pure and infinite freedom. As the gentle air caresses my skin, hesitation and fear evade me; for those unabating thoughts selfishly abandoned me some time ago.

Two. As years of desire culminate at this moment, the comforting warmth of the sun dwindles. There is, and always was, a clear expectation of cold. But this—this intoxication—is more than I imagined. More than I can, or want, to control. An instant addiction, and I crave it—no, demand it—as my body and mind yearn for more.

Three. As years of desire culminate at this moment, the numbing ravishes me with fury; immobilizing me, controlling me, owning me; I allow it, welcome it. Those which bind renounce their grasp, dissolving the suffering that encompasses my soul. Within the dimness, the calm approaches, luring me with the promise of freedom.

Four. As years of desire culminate at this moment, the fury yields to calm, and calm willingly accepts. The ripples and gentle curves, encircling the last lingering rays of light, fade to darkness as I embrace the deafening silence. Every fantasy sought-after and every dream coveted now unfetters. My eyes slowly seal and the waters bleed into me, claiming me as theirs.

Five. As years of desire conclude at this moment, five minutes achieves what I could not in a lifetime. I am finally free.

Mother and educator from New Hampshire, USA. Lover of all arts and arts integration. https://allpoetry.com/Fntsy_Rytr Allpoetry.com/Fntsy_Rytr

Putting my Pain Through Words

Forever searching for something to
numb myself so that I don't have
to deal with these hallucinations
do I really deserve the title of poet
when all I write are monstrosities
not golden masterpieces who is

There to trust other than my
perfect, clear lines and my playground
so rusted and worn by my own hands
I am so sick and tired of feeling
like this yet this is all I know
for I isolate too much but I

Can't seem to find a reason
to actually give a fuck forever
returning to the bottom of a bottle
and the arms of a sex partner
I know that I am a monster
and monsters don't get happy endings

I reach out to the gods only to get
completely ignored, I reach out
to friends only to be told that I
am on my own they say that

poetry holds the writer's heart
but what happens if your heart

Is encased in ice and dark, poisonous
ink feeling so sociopathic to the point
where I don't even care what happens
to me I am just sick of feeling this
mind numbing pain which is why
I act so stoic, so cold, so dark
it's better this way, trust me
nobody would even dare listen to
the story I once so easily told

———————————

Poetry helps me cope. Forgotten Poet writes with the stars.
Wolves howl at the moon. I normally write dark poetry.
However, I can also write light and happy poems. I listen to music
Allpoetry.com/Forgotten_Poet

[Na'im Abdallah]

Me and mine

I don't care what these people think or what they say, but what
they do
As long as it doesn't harm me and mine, well, that's fine too
But understand what I mean by me and mine
What that defines is more than just my family -- it's me and all my
kind
And I decline to be of those that's walking blind, when I see very
well
So I'm inclined to speak the truth, and unveil the lie in fairy tales

The first lie they told us, which we fell for was -- we were free
In a country that was based on justice, liberty, and equality;
But we never got an apology, never got compensation, and never
got treated properly;
They let us off plantations, but trapped us again with poverty;
You probably don't follow me, but I ain't trying to lead you
See! This is food for thought, all I'm trying to do is feed you;
If you don't want to eat it, that's fine; just leave it on the plate
For knowledge is abundant, but time I don't have none to waste

The biggest thing they told us that's false and most of y'all will
hate;
"Jesus is the Lord" is a lie, also a grave mistake,
And you can ask me why, and I will tell you the answer plain and
clear
Jesus was a man -- like you sitting there and me standing here

A messenger of God, who served God with complete submission;
But never did he say, "Worship me and be a Christian"
But what was told to us was in contradiction to what was written
This was an invention, established with the intention
For power and control in the form of religion
But you ain't trying to listen, you rather stay in the same
condition

Living in the matrix of legislators and politicians;
Law-breakers and lawmakers, racist snakes and crocodilians,
Smiling in your face but hatred is what the smile's concealin'
They claim to worship God; but in all actuality,
They oppose God, condoning homosexuality,
The mentality of these people is evil, corrupt and full of sin,
And it seems their war on terror also means war on black skin
They'll lock us up in prison for years for selling crack, man!
But there's no consequences when the police kills a black man

Yet, we thought it was all peaches and cream, and fell for the
scheme
Now we're trapped in their machine called 'The American Dream'
They paint the picture like it's something to be held in revere
I see the picture like - the quickest way to hell is living here
Turn the news on, all you ever hear is the worst
Because these people don't fear God and they never put him first;

Since we know that this problem makes this, what's the solution?
Resist and refuse to be a part of this pollution?
Retribution is for God, which shall come in His own time
So all I'm trying to do is -- just look out for me and mine...

I'd like to stay anonymous, hence the pen-name - Anonymous Kquote. I was born and raised in Oklahoma. My poetry is inspired from life's experiences and thoughts I have.
Allpoetry.com/Anonymous_kquote

Printed in Great Britain
by Amazon

79981870R00173